For the Grace of Joe

Vickie Morgan

ISBN-13: **978-1-989109-02-1**

For J, H, P and J. Without you, I would not be here.

AUTHOR'S NOTE

All the names in this book have been changed save for mine, Josh's and Joe's. If you want to know who any of them are in real life, send me an email. Also, if you are looking for a book about Trisomy 13 being a part of some master plan, this isn't it.

Chapter 1

I scheduled my 20-week ultrasound a few days early. My mother-in-law was supposed to come visit the following week from North Carolina and I wanted to limit the number of people in the room who didn't like me.

The night before I didn't give the screening a second thought. When I was pregnant with Cole they found an abnormality and offered us skads of genetic testing and suggested termination but we said no to all of it and everything turned out fine. Maybe the healthy toddler I had running around gave me a little confidence that the medical profession tended to overreact.

The Sandy Hook shooting was all over the news on the drive to the hospital. I looked in the back seat at my precious son and said, "We have everything we need right here in the car Josh. We are unbelievably lucky."

Our only thought going in was whether we'd find out if there was a boy or a girl on the way. We kept it a surprise on the first baby. He was out for five minutes before we even thought to ask because we were so busy crying and laughing and anxious to hear his Apgar score. The memory of lifting the baby off my chest to see who we were kissing and the medical team yelling "No! The baby is slippery, we'll check!" still made us chuckle.

Our conversation on that otherwise regular December morning was about how our Christmas might have been small and simple but compared to the parents who planned funerals in Newtown, Connecticut, we were more than fortunate.

As we drove under Tookey's Bridge on I-295 safely in Portland we agreed to have the doctor put the reveal in an envelope that we would leave closed unless we both decided to open it.

Chapter 2

Journal - December 28, 2012

Our ultrasound technician wasn't saying anything during the scan. I was asking what we were looking at and telling her what I had just learned in Biology 101. She had been moving around my belly with the wand for about 10 minutes and wasn't really smiling or responding so I asked if she was seeing ten fingers and toes on there. She zoomed in and showed me the baby's left hand and said, "Yup, there's a little thumb and four fingers...on that hand..." She put her hand on my leg. "I'm going to stop here to go get the doctor. There are some problems with your baby."

I glanced over at my calm husband and mouthed "I know right" and shook my head.

"What problems?" I asked.

Before she slipped out of the exam room she slowly and quietly told me there were issues with the kidneys, brain, heart, stomach, mouth, nose, jaw, feet, hands, the nuchal fold at the base of the baby's neck and the intestines.

I sat there in my paper gown and stared at the wall. I reached for my cellphone to call my aunt Caroline back in Newfoundland. She knew we had an appointment and was waiting for the good report. She immediately asked what was wrong. I told her probably nothing. The doctors were just freaking out over nothing just like the last time. I'll call you back when this is all cleared up.

When the doctor we had never met before came in the room, he stood way too close to me and talked so low I could barely hear him. He said we were probably looking at a chromosomal abnormality for there to be so many issues. I felt heat traveling up my arms and legs. I wondered if he was ever going to try and make me feel better by saying it was all a joke and this wasn't truly happening. But he didn't.

I asked Mr. Lab Coat to tell us what the technician had been unable to determine. Were we having a boy or a girl. He turned the machine on and put the wand on my belly and dug it in at a few different angles and told me no, he couldn't. As he flipped the switch back off, he explained this was normal for babies who had chromosomal abnormalities to have ambiguous genitals. And besides, it was just so early.

He told us our fetus would likely be so delayed and

deformed if it did survive that we should consider our options for continuing the pregnancy.

The baby was kicking me while the doctor was talking so I got hung up on the word fetus. We had just seen the cardiac rhythms on the monitor from the beating heart. I made a crack about our expectations for our children and that we didn't want them to grow up to be doctors anyway.

Nobody laughed.

There was now a genetic counselor in the room along with the specialist and they wanted to keep talking but I didn't trust either one of them. I waved my arms for them all to stop and asked if we could have some time. I wanted the full report sent to my OB/GYN and we would take some time to talk this over as a family.

Chapter 3

I felt a wave of guilt for not staying up all night the night
before the screening to imagine all the bad possibilities. I
told myself this is exactly what you get for taking things for
granted. And for scheduling this when you knew Mary Ann
couldn't intrude. I remembered every insensitive joke I had
ever made. When I got dehydrated a few weeks earlier I told
someone my baby would probably come out with six fingers
on each hand. And sweet Jesus when I used to work in the
bakery at Dominion years ago and a customer was taking
too long coming up with something to write on a baby
shower cake, I made a crack to a coworker that I should
have written 'Hope your baby isn't stillborn.' Ugh and that
time Mom had to tell me to stop using the word retarded
around my cousin because she had a brother with Down
Syndrome. This was all my fault for being such a shitty
person.

I don't recall the ride home. Or sleeping that night. Or going
to the airport to pick up my son's grandmother and great

grandmother the next day. We had asked them to stay at a hotel when they booked their flights a month earlier so it was already tense.

They had sent about 40 random unwrapped gifts ahead of time. I wrapped it all and put it under our tree. I assumed they would want to see Cole's reactions and I wouldn't let him open anything from them until they arrived.

I asked if anyone wanted a cup of tea and neither of them said yes. In Newfoundland you'd accept tea in your worst enemy's kitchen and maybe even become friends if they had good biscuits. We don't speak the same language.

We sat and took pictures while our 2-year-old pulled all the wrapping paper off. Some of the gifts were nice and some of it was dangerous cheap crap that just made me angry. I wanted them to go home.

For some reason the hotel reservation didn't include their first night in town so we agreed it was easier for them to just crash on the couch. They complained about being cold and there weren't enough pillows but it was in that Southern way of reassuring you that it was okay while pointing it out at the same time. My mother-in-law mentioned their bad backs but we're fine, go to bed. We'll see you in the morning.

Upstairs in our room, I wanted to talk to Josh about how we would handle the next week of waiting for more information while we were entertaining guests. There was no way I could keep up that stupid grin and pretend we were going to have a new baby. At least not the baby they wanted. No, it was time to tell them that my baby was going to have some problems and that we were all going to have to get used to the idea of a child with a cleft lip and special needs.

Chapter 4

I used to have a friend whose son and husband had cleft lip
and she had told me once about how beautiful the baby's
smile was before the surgery. This was so long before any of
this was a factor in my life and I had asked if she was
concerned about how he would look when she found out.
Abby told me Shane's face would literally just open up when
he was happy and she almost didn't want to get the
corrective procedure. It wouldn't have hurt him to leave it
alone and she reminded me that her husband had the scar
as well and figured he would just look that much more like
his Dad so no, she wasn't concerned.

Shane was 15 when I met him and he was tall, handsome
and talented. His twin brother Trevor had a job to keep up
with him physically and socially. Josh and I were volunteers
at a theater where Abby worked and watched her twin boys
thriving. They were both lead actors in the theatre
productions and Shane even had a girlfriend.

By the time I got pregnant with a baby who had a cleft palate

I hadn't talked to Abby for a number of years but her approach to her son's 'deformity' was inspiring and stayed with me.

Chapter 5

We sat down for breakfast the next morning with Josh's mom and grandmother and I started in. Josh was bringing food to the table that we had cooked together in our tiny kitchen and he kept sending me supportive looks over their heads. I didn't have an ultrasound picture to show them like they had hoped and I explained that we had gone to our appointment but we had some news to share. Josh still wasn't sitting down so I tried to coach them on the reaction I wanted to see. That we would get through as a family.

And then I told them we had some news about the baby.

My mother-in-law started wringing her hands into her paper towel napkin. My grandmother-in-law kept looking out the window nodding and saying mmm hmmmm. Her head was moving slower than usual and she seemed to be having trouble swallowing her food.

It wasn't quite what I was hoping for with the no words or emotions so I pushed onward. I explained that we had been offered an abortion but we demanded the doctor never use that word again around us because this baby was a part of our lives and we would love him/her no matter what.

There were tepid nods of agreement. Josh sat down and I kept talking.

We need to keep things normal for Cole since he has no concept of special needs or that this is in any way not what was supposed to happen so if you guys could help us in that way, this will be a normal part of *his* life and we'll teach him to stand up for and protect his sibling just like we will.

Stunned silence.

Josh could see that I was out of words. He took over and reiterated what I had said about how we were going to approach the rest of this pregnancy and the tears started flowing around the table. We love you and we'll do whatever you need and you can get through this. It was heartwarming.

I helped Cole with his breakfast.

Chapter 6

By December 31, we had been driving around looking at the same sights and looking for the same antique shops for days. I was delegated to the back seat of our small SUV with one of our visitors and a car seat holding Cole wedged between us. Our other visitor claimed my passenger side seat up front. MeeMaw basically raised Josh so having her up there was really good *for them* and it was out of necessity more than anything since I was the only one that could fit behind my giant husband's seat. I stopped going in to the shops with them and instead elected to stay in the truck and blast the music and pretend I was somewhere else.

The conversations were so normal and I couldn't seem to get hold of a doctor who could prescribe me anything that was effective for nausea and anxiety but also considered safe for a pregnant lady. I felt like everyone was angry at me. Not so much for feeling shitty but for being so selfish that I was asking for relief.

We pulled into a Tim Horton's parking lot and I just burst out of the vehicle to get some air. I noticed MeeMaw was looking a little piqued and holding a table to steady herself. She was feeling sickly too and we realized we had been driving around for hours without food and her blood sugar was low and she hadn't taken her insulin. I put an arm around her and said well no wonder we feel like crap, let's get some food in us.

After we had eaten we headed to the grocery store to get ingredients for the birthday party the next day. I got a recipe from MeeMaw for those tiny baked ham sandwiches my mother-in-law loved and there would be mac and cheese, chocolate cake, rice krispie treats, cocktail weenies...it was going to be very nice. We were going to spend the evening with delicious smells around the house and watch the countdown on television or even drive downtown to see the fireworks. We told Cole the whole world was counting down the seconds to his birthday.

We had invited my police officer friend and her kids over to celebrate with Cole the next afternoon. Gail Conway was my self-defense instructor the first time I took the Rape Aggression Defense class and she became my mentor when I took the instructor training. She had thrown a baby shower for me when I was pregnant with Cole and she was more a part of our family than anyone I had hoped to see that

Christmas. I felt safe and empowered when she was around and I couldn't wait to see her.

Around five in the evening, our extended family members decided to go back to their motel room and asked if we could drive them. Cole and I stayed in the kitchen working on the preparations while Josh drove them to Freeport. It was pretty slippery by then so on the way home he got pizza for our dinner. We watched Christmas movies by ourselves and watched the ball drop in Times Square from the comfort of our living room like everybody else who is having a baby who might die and is trying to keep things normal for the little boy who is excited to get his New Year's Day birthday cake.

Chapter 7

Just before the final push, Dr. Porter asked me to reach down and feel the top of the baby's head. I had refused the mirror to watch the proceedings and I had been in hard yowling labour for 36 hours. I was exhausted. Josh was exhausted. The nurses had insisted we walk the halls and climb the stairs again and again to keep labour going. At one point they asked if Josh would promise to stimulate my nipples if they left the room. They offered a massage with essential oils and that sounded nice until a nurse that didn't look all that clean came in with half used bottles of stuff that looked like it lived in her medicine cabinet at home. I asked her to leave.

When Cole arrived Josh cut the cord and the baby was placed on my belly. I managed to keep him there for about 25 minutes with a Neonatal Intensive Care Unit (NICU) team staring at me before they took him from my arms. I asked Josh to go with them while I got cleaned up.

Five hours later I called the NICU to see when my baby

would be returned to me. Someone was gone to lunch and the lady on the phone didn't have time to do the paperwork to release him because she was too busy.

We went to NICU to find my son not only bathed against my written request, but he was also sucking on a pacifier. I questioned the attending nurse and she said "Well he was all covered in that schmook so I cleaned him. And the pacifier stopped the crying."

Chapter 8

In the early afternoon of New Year's Day 2013, Gail arrived with her two kids wearing their best Christmas outfits. Charles looked like such a little man with his vest and clip-on tie and Shannen was a tiny princess. They had brought gifts for Cole and a card for us that had a handmade coupon inside for a free newborn photo session. Cole's package had a John Deere t-shirt that said "Best Big Bro" and I froze for what felt like a very long time. I looked at my friend and mentor who had scratched my itchy nose through a face shield and talked me through my whitest fear during simulation in self-defense class. She knew something was wrong. I shook my head. She took in a fast breath and I saw her eyes get damp. I smiled at her and gestured at the kids playing on the floor and she smiled back as best she could.

I brought out all the food Josh and I had prepared the night before and laid it out on the table and on top of the deep freeze that was also in the dining room. Gail stood beside me making plates for her kids while my mother-in-law and grandmother-in-law announced they would get leftovers out of the fridge so as not to waste them. The microwave beeped as they reheated food from two days prior and they sat across from me eating stuff I hadn't had a chance to throw out.

My living room then became an interrogation room as my friend and mother-in-law got to know each other. All of a sudden police work was fascinating and every detail of how we met and how much time we spent together became of utmost importance. Officer Conway had her work face back on when we made eye contact across the room. I knew she had dealt with many similar personalities before so I focused on playing with the kids.

When it was time to go home I helped my mom friend get the kids' jackets and boots on. I was struggling to find proper parting words so I decided to walk them out. I was standing beside their car when I realized I had not brought a jacket.

As her kids waited in the car, I told Gail what they had said at the doctor's office. IF I have made it to term and IF the baby was born alive, the health problems would be almost unbearable and the life expectancy was just a few months. All the markers were there for a Trisomy chromosomal abnormality and we wouldn't know more until we saw the doctor….the doctor who had delivered my first baby and her two babies that we both trusted. It was a nightmare. Standing there with Gail the diagnosis felt real and I couldn't stop crying or hugging my friend. She kept telling her kids to wait one more minute. It was almost good that it was so cold because it kept me present. I was in the presence of someone who was safe for me that would actually comfort me and love my baby no matter what. I needed that.

When I finally came back inside my lips were blue and I couldn't feel my hands. My mother-in-law was standing in front of the living room window overlooking the parking lot holding my son. She said he wanted to see where Mom went. She couldn't wait to show me that she had taught him to kiss her on the lips. The pictures her mom took of the kissing lesson ended up on Facebook as her profile picture. It's good to remember and mark where you were during those big moments.

Chapter 9

When I was pregnant with Cole the doctors suspected he had tuberous sclerosis because of a blip on an ultrasound in my 32nd week. Genetic counselors and high risk obstetric specialists swarmed us and warned us that getting tested ourselves was the only responsible thing to do. We were told that Cole would have multiple cognitive delays and lots of scary health problems and that it likely came from us. They strongly suggested an abortion. At 32 weeks.

They started calling the blip a tumour because "that's what they call something when they don't know what it is." The professional in front of me shrugged and said it was just a scientific term as though she had never heard of cancer before.

We didn't get tested. We didn't do further testing on Cole other than extra ultrasounds to monitor the blip. We rode out the pregnancy and hoped for the best. The doctors told me for the safety of the baby I shouldn't take any pain medication during delivery because it might make him drowsy and they could misinterpret his responsiveness. They warned me that he would immediately be taken from me and up to NICU for observation and that the NICU team would want to observe the birth.

After he arrived Cole was put under an ultraviolet light to see if he had skin lesions associated with tuberous sclerosis. He didn't. He was given an ultrasound on his liver and kidneys to look for signs. There weren't any. We left the hospital with orders to have an ultrasound of his brain sometime before the fontanels closed over to avoid more invasive tests.

I refused that last one because I had given in to the other tests despite having a perfectly healthy, thriving child.

When Cole was a little over a year old the doctors were still on us about the prenatal blip and refused to admit they overreacted. Our pediatrician called me at home and advised me that it was against his recommendation to skip the brain scan. He said that since he was Cole's advocate, he had to insist on what was best for Cole. At the time I thought he was a good doctor for taking such an active and aggressive role in my child's care.

I stayed up all night worrying about what the neurologist might find during the ultrasound on Cole's fontanel. I worried about the gamma rays being able to pass through the soft spot and slowing the growth of brain cells that would likely mean he'd forget how to breathe or walk at some point. I kept watching to make sure his fingers could grasp small objects and panicked when he couldn't and would go look up what a baby should be able to do at this age. I considered what all this anxiety was doing to my body and if I was basically contaminating the breast milk supply with cortisol by having so many panic attacks.

As soon as we met the neurologist he measured Cole's head with a strip of tape like I had in my sewing kit back at the house. Josh was holding our firstborn in his lap so the doctor then measured Josh's head. Dr. Brainiac said they had the exact same ratio of head size to their body size. He told us he didn't need to do the ultrasound because he was reasonably certain there was normal brain growth. He said pediatricians often overreact to growth patterns because their guidelines are on the ultra-conservative side.

Old Doctor PushyPants prodded us on Cole's care a few more times before we fired him and found another person to be our child's health advocate.

Chapter 10

On January 3rd we made a trip to Sam's Club in Scarborough with my mother-in-law while MeeMaw stayed behind. I had deduced that my baby was a girl in spite of the doctor's claim that there was ambiguous genitals. When Cole was scanned at 20 weeks they could see he was a boy and just didn't tell me so I assumed the ambiguity was actually an absence of something definitive and so I declared that this was a girl.

In the checkout aisle we were beside a family that had two grown children with Downs Syndrome. They were letting the kids put food up on the belt just like we were doing with Cole. The Mom and Dad would guide their hands when they got distracted and shush them when they spoke too loudly and helped them zip up their coats.

I stood frozen in place holding the scrapbook kit I had found with all the pink papers and borders and stickers in it. My mother-in-law came back and stood beside me and put her arm around my shoulders and said "Don't you worry, we're going to take care of our baby." She took the kit out of my hands and paid for it and handed it back to me.

I could no longer look at families with children who had special needs and be thankful that my child was typical. I would have to learn to clean feeding tubes and breathing tubes and watch my second born be wheeled off on a stretcher to multiple life-saving and life-threatening surgeries.

Josh lead me out of the store. I was in hell. But I had Grace and she needed me.

Chapter 11

Journal - January 4, 2013

We considered getting a second opinion. Maybe go to Boston or to the Catholic hospital in town so maybe they wouldn't be so quick to offer an abortion. We have already been to the best facility in the state. If we went to a less-equipped place, they would refer us right back to where we had gone already. Boston would tell us the same thing. We needed more information and despite our vow to never set foot in the hospital again - we went back.

There's a blood test they can do on me called MaterniT21. It's only being performed by a lab in California and it takes two weeks to get the results. It's intended to look for Trisomy 21 which is Down Syndrome. When the baby's blood cells break down, some of the DNA material comes out in my blood. They can also look for Trisomy 18 (Edwards Syndrome) and Trisomy 13 (Patau Syndrome).

What I can find online is that the test is most accurate at detecting Trisomy 21. A little less accurate for Trisomy 18 and less accurate for Trisomy 13 but still about 92% accurate.

Babies with Edwards Syndrome are not expected to survive more than a week. Babies with Patau Syndrome are given about a year at best. There is a range of severity with these conditions - partial, mosaic and full. Some babies get all the markers for their condition and others get less.

I can't find a definitive answer on how fatal this might be. There are kids with a full Trisomy that survive. Some just have a partial Trisomy and still don't make it.

Chapter 12

I went to have the blood drawn for the MaterniT21. While we sat in the waiting room Cole was playing a kids colouring app on our tablet. A lumpy female of advanced years sitting next to us muttered that kids these days are ruined because they wouldn't know what a real crayon looks like.

I wanted to tell her that Cole colours at home all the time but since we were there to find out how long our new baby might live, I didn't want to bring crayons that I'd have to chase all over the floor. I said nothing. I rolled my eyes at my husband who didn't see because he was rolling his eyes at me at the same time.

The lab technician was friendly and didn't ask a lot of questions about the test. In fact he kept me off the subject altogether. I think his name was Justin. He didn't divulge any secret way to rig the test or how to get out of this diagnosis. He looked like he could help but he just did his job. On the way back to the car, I sent Josh and Cole on ahead and called my OB/GYN's office. He was out for a few days to celebrate the holiday with his family. He alternated Christmases with his business partner Dr. Wagner and had probably just spent the last few days with women delivering New Year's babies that took 36 hours to emerge.

The on-call doctor's assistant was friendly enough. I tried explaining that I needed a prescription for some anxiety medication to be called in. The assistant had concerns that I was 20 weeks pregnant and was reluctant to call anything in without consulting my regular OB/GYN. I held myself up with a wall in the lobby and started crying uncontrollably. "I'm waiting on test results to see how long this baby I'm carrying will live and I need something to help me breathe."

A few minutes later her office called back. Dr. Wagner had called in a script for a two week supply of 1 mg Ativan. I had only asked for two or three pills at half that dose but Dr. Wagner said that if she were in my shoes, she'd need a hell of a lot more than what she prescribed to get through. She told her secretary to tell me to go home and take care of myself as best I could and try to hang in there.

Finally a person who saw what we were facing and seemed to have a clue about how it felt to be incubating a palliative care unit.

Chapter 13

Waiting for the results of the MaterniT21 was torture. I lived on the internet searching and researching. One minute I would feel strong enough to read the facts and the next I'd go back to the Rick Santorum story because his daughter appeared to be doing great. There were online groups for post-diagnosis support but none for expectant parents. We might after all not be a part of the club and imagine how bad we'd look if we had to say "our baby's fine, sorry about your kids though."

The loss groups were too far past where we were and I hoped to never join them.

I talked to the genetic counselor when I went in for the blood test. I had found an article about what their job really is. They are the fluffers for the OB/GYNs. They tell patients the hard information laced with suggestions on what most other people choose to do. There are urban legends that 95% of people terminate after they get confirmation of Trisomy 13, 18 and 21.

Paula Collins confirmed all the information I had found online about Patau, Edwards and Down syndromes. She told Dr. Porter that her guess was Trisomy 13 but that Trisomy 18 was a strong possibility. I wanted to know where we could learn how to clean the tubes and machines that we would need for the baby - whether that was something she had referrals for or if the hospital would teach us. Did we need to buy clothes that allowed for easy access to the tubes.

She said that to expect a baby with Trisomy 13 to live past one year was optimistic and that six months was more likely. Babies with Trisomy 18 have a life expectancy of six months with one week being more realistic. She warned me that with either diagnosis we would probably never take the baby home from the hospital and that was only if we made it to full term. We heard that phrase a lot. It was as if the professionals were afraid we might get our hopes up and then sue them if the baby didn't make it. "Incompatible with life." That was another phrase we heard again and again.

It was about 7:00 in the evening when Dr. Porter called me at home. His voice was so soothing. He called me Victoria. He told me my baby had Trisomy 13.

I asked if the test had confirmed what I suspected - that my baby was a girl. He said he honestly couldn't remember as the paperwork was back at his office. He just knew it said positive for Trisomy 13. I was a little angry that the important information was the diagnosis and not which name we might have to put on a grave.

He told me I sounded upbeat.

It was like an accusation. As though I hadn't asked Josh to push me over the stairs to put an end to the nightmare. As though I had slept in the last 20-something days.

I took what is called a ragged breath like Reba's mother in the Night the Lights Went out in Georgia. I told him that in the lottery of Trisonomies, at least we had the better one. He was silent. Because, I continued, I've been thinking the baby had Trisonomy 18 which would be worse. At least we get more time. This kid is a fighter Dr. Porter and Grace chose us and this isn't a mistake. We're going to do everything we can to meet her, right Dr. Porter?

Nobody had the guts to tell me I was saying Trisomy wrong or that it was Fancy's Mom.

Chapter 14

Journal - January 17, 2013

Dr. Porter had been doing some research since he called me at home last week. At my appointment he showed me a report that says a lot of the medical profession is of the opinion that these babies are not worth saving but that this attitude is not universally accepted because when there are interventions, there are success stories.

We discuss the options before us. I have taken abortion off the table and it has now been labelled medical termination even though my health is not in jeopardy. Once we establish that my partner and my doctor and I are in this for as long as nature allows - we have two options left. Plan for delivery and decide to do nothing. Or do something/everything in our power to keep this baby alive after the birth.

I was sitting on the comically high exam table swinging my legs and talking about what a fighter my little Grace was going to be and Dr. Porter got a funny look on his face. He opened my chart and passed me a piece of paper. It was the test results from Sequenom. I glanced down through and said "What should I be looking at?"

He said, "Victoria, that's the test results from the MaterniT21. It says whether you're having a boy or a girl."

At the bottom of the page it said Y chromosome positive. No problem for a science genius like me. I took Biology two times after all just a year before that but for some reason my brain couldn't formulate a Punnett square and I said, "Yeah, Y-chromosome, that's a girl."

"No Victoria, you're having a boy."

I had been imagining a little girl that everybody would look at because of her cleft lip and small chin and various tubes. When I pictured a little boy, for some reason I thought he had a better chance. That it wouldn't matter nearly as much how he looked and that somehow he'd be physically tougher.

"Well I guess we have to come up with a new name then."

I walked out of the appointment with renewed hope. The baby was kicking up a storm and my heart felt lighter. We just needed more information to prepare for what lay ahead.

I asked for a full body, head to toe scan, no interruptions, no advice, just a full report on whether anything had changed from the 18-week ultrasound. I wanted a DVD copy of the scan and I wanted pictures like they give you when your baby counts.

I also made an appointment with the only pediatric cardiologist in the state who does fetal heart ultrasound scans. The biggest concern is the baby's heart. Everything else seems to be irrelevant if the heart won't work so let's start from there.

Chapter 15

When we were expecting Cole we went to a birthing class at Birth Roots in Portland, Maine. We were determined to make the best possible decisions for our baby and explored any information we could find. We met a couple who were in their 40s who were expecting their first baby. We talked about testing for abnormalities. At that point I hadn't given much consideration to testing. I didn't want a needle poked into my pregnant belly I knew that for sure. I was looking forward to ultrasounds but mostly for the pictures. I knew my general practitioner ran a host of tests that required nine vials of blood the second we found out I was pregnant but they were mostly to check on my health.

I didn't want to run tests with any risks to the baby. Mostly because we didn't care one way or the other if something was wrong.

Around 10 weeks there's generally an ultrasound for due date and viability. This is the part where couples are often devastated to find out there is no heartbeat. That can happen for a multitude of reasons and they are sent home to wait for the miscarriage to happen. Or if you're really lucky, there's a heartbeat and they measure the tiny little curvy mass on the screen and tell you about when the baby should arrive. Aside from the positive pregnancy test, this is the first real confirmation that your family is growing and it's okay to start making plans. In another month the morning sickness might even stop and you may even get a few months of comfort before the last trimester which has a host of other crap to contend with like heartburn and gestational diabetes and peeing every 20 minutes.

I turned down early testing on Cole and felt confident about it. We didn't seem to have a choice on Joe. The genetic counselor believed he had Trisomy 13. The MaterniT21 was presumed to be the next logical step. Paula Collins stood beside the doctor as he told me me my baby had ambiguous genitals and would likely die.

The research I did in 2013 about the MaterniT21 said that it was almost 92% accurate and there was minimal chance of false positives (where it comes back positive but is wrong). That hasn't changed. To my knowledge, even a positive test would need to be confirmed by an amniocentesis before they would proceed with a termination.

Nobody gave us brochures on services for kids with special needs or support groups for parents when the results came in. In other words, they go in looking for something among babies who they already have a good idea have something wrong. If they're wrong or right, the doctors make money like they do from any other pharmaceutical company. In fact this organization that does the testing has been given exclusive access to high risk pregnancies to run this test. Not research of course, just as a service.

It is almost globally available. It used to be just one company in California who ran this test. It has expanded. Who it is offered to and which insurance companies will cover it is supposed to be based on risk and history. You can also pay for it out of pocket if you are willing to travel for it.

Chapter 16

Journal - February 1, 2013

The baby hasn't kicked me more than twice in two days. That's what the doctors have told me to look for to determine how the baby is doing.

If there is a death in utero, the baby will not deliver spontaneously. I will have to go see if there is a heartbeat at the doctor's office, then over to the hospital for an ultrasound to be sure there's no heartbeat and then labour would be induced. Unless there is a normal, pregnancy-related cause for a C-section, I will have to deliver the baby like any other pregnancy. We are already well beyond the point of bleeding and cramps and suffering through it at home. This is a fully-formed, dilation necessary before he comes out, baby.

On the way to the OB/GYN's office, I'm scheduling everything in my mind. Okay, if I have to go get induced tonight, the person who will be taking care of my son is available and I'll probably be in the hospital all weekend. I'll tell my professors what's going on and I might even finish out this semester at university.

I had no pictures of the baby and everything was unknown except for a too-early ultrasound that showed most everything was wrong.

My OB/GYN found the heart beating just fine. The heart rate was a little slower than it had been but it's still strong. We're doing okay. Just get through the weekend and go to the next couple of ultrasounds and see where we are.

In the meantime, I asked about CPM - Confined Placental Mosaicism. I found out about a condition where the placenta had the chromosomal abnormality and the baby was fine. There was a story online about a woman who found out at 20 weeks that her baby had enlarged kidneys. The MaterniT21 test came back positive for Trisomy 13. She had an amniocentesis that said her baby was fine. She was due to deliver a few weeks ago.

That could happen to me right? I could be that one in a million women who gets a positive result from this so-called foolproof test and it's just something wrong with my placenta.

Dr. Porter had never heard of it but guessed that the

ultrasound in that lady's case hadn't indicated any problems and there was reason to doubt the MaterniT21 result.

Well....yeah.....but.....

Just wishful thinking I guess.

Chapter 17

The report from the December ultrasound said our baby had (from head to toe) extra space around the brain, cleft palate, small jaw, thickening of the nuchal fold at the base of the neck, polydactyly (extra finger on each hand, extra toe on each foot), a heart defect, bright kidneys (this meant they were not functioning or had calcified), omphalocele (intestines herniated into the umbilical cord) and rocker bottom feet. Even though the scan was only 10 minutes instead of the normal 45, the report said the baby's stomach wasn't filling and emptying which meant the baby wasn't swallowing amniotic fluid as should be expected.

What I knew going into this scan was the difference between 6 mm and 6.4 mm is very small so the nuchal fold wasn't THAT big and it was just a measurement on a moving baby that was only 18 weeks along. Plus the baby was lying prone (on the belly) the whole time. The cleft palate and omphalocele are very fixable. Babies only learn to swallow at around 23 weeks so to expect it five weeks prior was ridiculous.

The ultrasound technician this time around was wonderful. She said the kidneys were still showing up a little large but no longer bright. The baby was swallowing and the kidneys were functioning. The growth had been right on target at the prior scan and gave me the exact due date of May 24 (Victoria Day in Canada) that we expected. The current scan showed the baby was growing at around the 20th percentile. That's the exact opposite of my first baby who was consistently at the 80th percentile or higher.

Essentially, most babies grow at around the 50th percentile or average growth. My giant firstborn son grew way faster and bigger. This child is growing slower and smaller.

We got some great pictures. We mistakenly asked for 3D pictures. At 24 weeks, even babies who are developing perfectly look like birds. That was not the way to ease our minds. But the rest of the ultrasound was encouraging.

Chapter 18

February 5, 2013

12:15 pm

I arrive at the pediatric cardiologist's office. I'm ushered into a room right away. I stayed up all night last night worrying so we should be okay today.

1:15 pm

Doctor enters and apologizes for having me sit there with no television or magazines like the cozy waiting room offered. No big deal. It's not like I have much on my mind. An hour of silence was just what I needed to get me closer to full on psychosis. My partner was in the car with our sleeping, teething toddler.

I tell the doctor he can make it up to me by giving me a perfectly formed 24 week baby heart report.

He warns me that he doesn't talk during the scan but will tell me when he's finished what he sees.

He proceeds to do the ultrasound with his hand rested on my pelvic bone. He gestures from left to right like a windshield wiper as he moves the wand but the heat from his touch starts to make my skin crawl. I realize he needs to just focus on one small area and perhaps the baby is rested down low in my hips and maybe his hand is tired but there's no nurse or assistant in there with us. This doctor in a position of power made sure I knew it.

He's brought a sheet of paper like you would give a kid to colour. It's got a picture of a newborn baby drawn on there and a dumbed-down version of a heart. He draws on it while he talks.

The baby has a left superior vena cava. No big deal. Lots of people have those he tells me. It just drains into the heart and blood flow carries on as normal. The chambers are all perfect. The valves are all perfect. The septum that separates the heart which I'm expecting to be the problem is perfect. The aorta however is measuring a little small.

While I'm still pregnant and the baby doesn't need to get oxygen through the lungs, it's not a big deal. After birth, they will take the baby, do an echocardiogram and determine if there is in fact a coarctation. If there is, the pressure will increase on the aorta and the weak spot will begin to pinch off and eventually stop supplying oxygen to the stomach, lungs and brain. There's a tube type area that can alleviate the pressure but the medication that helps this happen causes babies to forget to breathe. Given that my baby will likely forget to breathe anyway (doctor's words not mine) this medication is not recommended.

There is a surgery that will correct the coarctation. They go in through the baby's ribs and snip the pinchy part of the aorta and stitch it up (Sorry for the technical jargon).

It's invasive and takes a long time to heal but will essentially fix the problem permanently.

Okay, so we're out of the woods.

"...but I don't advise you to have this surgery on your baby..."

I had read about families who met doctors who advised against life-sustaining surgery. I really didn't expect to meet any of them.

I must have appeared to not understand so he gave me an analogy.

Imagine you had bought a house. You get in there and it has numerous problems but you figure you can get them fixed. One guy will tell you oh I can take care of the asbestos. Another guy will assure you he can fix the plumbing. Someone else will tell you not to worry about the electrical. But at the end of the day, the house is not worth it. In other words, between the omphalocele and the cleft palate and the developmental delays this baby will undoubtedly have, well, you know.

I sat there dumbstruck for a minute and replied "I don't think you can compare the value of a rundown house to a baby's life. If anything, that story only reflects how little value the doctors in Maine place on a child with special needs."

So then he arrived at the real reason for his recommendation to not get this surgery. In his experience, the surgeons capable of doing the procedure will not touch a baby with Trisomy 13.

There is a possibility of having a stent inserted into the problem area. It could help for hours, days, weeks, even years. If we have the real surgery, the baby may not be accessible and we could be deprived of the time we would have had if we had opted for the bandaid solution.

So do we find a hospital willing to do the surgery? Should I move to North Carolina - the place they nicknamed the Research Triangle? Maybe they would be happy to take a chance on a child if it might increase their 'miracles worked' numbers. Maybe I could move back to Canada and find a hospital that will work on a child with a Trisomy 13 diagnosis.

I have four more months of pregnancy to find a solution. My baby is one pound, two ounces right now. How accurate is the measurement of the aorta? What if the doctor is wrong about the diagnosis?

It's all bargaining. And it means a hell of a lot of work rewriting the book on Trisomy 13 in Maine.

We went home and watched our ultrasound video and imagined what it would be like to hold the baby's hand even for a minute.

Chapter 19

The report my OB/GYN received from the head toe to scan indicated no changes from prior scan even though Joe was swallowing fluid and the kidneys weren't glowing as bright which I assumed showed improvement and possibly took kidney transplants and dialysis off the table. The baby was kicking constantly and a baby with a Trisomy 13 diagnosis is not supposed to be active. Not to mention the fact that I was still pregnant. I considered all of those details to be good signs.

Cole was cutting four molars and was screaming on my shoulder while I talked to Dr. Porter. I remembered to bring the piece of construction paper with the heart picture on it from the cardiologist's office and explained what was told to me as best as I could.

I asked if what Dr. PelvicThrust had said was true. That heart surgeries were not performed on children diagnosed with Trisomy 13 at Maine Med.

In his ever-diplomatic way, Dr. Porter said he wasn't aware of a refusal to do surgery so much as a lack of opportunity. There just haven't been any babies with Trisomy 13 or Trisomy 18 to operate on. Most either don't make it because of miscarriage or more often there is a medical termination soon after the diagnosis is confirmed.

He had been at the same hospital for more than 25 years.

Chapter 20

I had never considered university as a possibility until I learned about student loans and by then my grades weren't high enough to get in at Memorial University.

After I graduated high school I went to night school for math and English classes to boost my application. I wanted a degree in Psychology. At first it was music but my high school band teacher was concerned I might lose my aspiration for higher education when I saw how hard music school was to get in to. I eventually spent four semesters at MUN before flunking out. I was 19.

When Josh was 19 he had already been in the Air Force for two years. He served for six years altogether and deployed three times to the Middle East.

It was on a return from one of those deployments that his flight crew found themselves in St. John's, Newfoundland, and bumped into a local lady who was happy to meet someone who had not ever read her hockey wedding planning columns in The Telegram.

We got married five months later and at first we tried living in Canada. I had two minimum wage jobs and had weaseled my way into an apartment in public housing. With my previous education at that point I was qualified to do entry level secretarial work that I hated doing. Josh didn't have a Canadian work permit so he couldn't work at all and within a year we were volunteering at the food bank to alleviate the guilt of visiting the food bank. We packed up and moved to the States.

I got a work permit fairly quickly but with my spotty resume and unique accent, I was just adding to my list of George Costanza-style exits from various companies. Josh landed a job with Time Warner Cable in North Carolina where he worked for that first year. I was busy finding out the real reason folks are so religious in the Bible Belt - the rampant racism and homophobia combined with the God-awful heat terrifies everyone when they realize Hell might be hotter and they better get to repentin'. Bless their hearts. It wasn't a good fit for me.

One night in Greensboro we were watching a Steve Carell movie that looked like it had been shot in Maine. I said it might be nice to move to Maine and maybe meet Stephen

King one day.

Five years later we had more sob stories on our resumes, an 18-month old baby and dreams of a better life. Josh had moved on to the call center at Time Warner and hated it. He was getting yelled at all day long about billing discrepancies and eating Tylenol for the never-subsiding headache that settled behind his eyebrows.

Josh's time in the Air Force entitled him to the GI Bill but he hesitated to use it because he hadn't ever gone to college before. He had wanted to be an English teacher since he was in high school. As a permanent resident I qualified for Pell grants, so we went back to school.

So it was while I was pregnant with a baby who had been diagnosed with Trisomy 13 that I found myself in a Psychology class at University of Southern Maine. It was a required class and only one guy taught it. It was all about eyeballs and ear hammers and lab tests on the sensory system of rats. I had been showing for a while and was navigating my belly around frat boys and sorority girls and propping my feet up while I took notes that made my stomach churn. I thought it best to let my professor know what was happening.

I had another required Psych class with a professor who

gave me options to accommodate any and all possibilities with the pregnancy.

The other professor (the eyeball guy) hadn't returned any of my emails.

Chapter 21

Journal - February 7, 2013

My therapist has been survival planning with me. Sometimes we talk about what would happen if there was a 'fetal demise in utero.' Sometimes I go into his office unable to breathe and my favourite chair feels like it's hanging from the ceiling.

I have been learning breathing techniques online on how to return to the room and listen to what we are talking about. He reminds me that when I planned this pregnancy I told him that Josh and Cole and I were so happy that we could handle just about anything.

We talk about who has been in touch since the gossip must have surely moved through my family and friends back home.

A few notable people have been oddly quiet and when I call home to Newfoundland I test the waters by saying "I know a lot of people think I should just terminate and get this over with." The silence tells me I am right on the money. I can almost hear what they're thinking. Just another thing Vickie is doing for attention when she could just have an abortion and put this child out of its misery. She's so goddamned selfish.

Chapter 22

I worried about who would take care of Cole when I had to deliver Joe. I wanted Josh with me since he had literally been at my side for every single contraction on my first baby. Dr. Porter told him that night in the delivery room that we should teach parenting classes because Josh had been the perfect support person. The thought of doing any of this without him there terrified me.

Ideally we needed a person we trusted to come stay with Cole when we went to the hospital or even come along with us.

Someone suggested that the other self-defense instructors I volunteered my time with ought to start spending time with Cole so that he would be comfortable staying with one of them when I went into labour.

Someone else offered to come stay with us should the unthinkable happen. She added that she would prefer to come when I went ahead and scheduled the 'other option.'

It wasn't as if I didn't reach out for help. We even considered inviting Josh's mom to come stay with us and I'm sure she would have been on the next plane but I didn't want to leave Cole alone with her.

One of the nights I had rushed into the hospital thinking Cole was on the way we had been on the labour and delivery floor and heard a toddler's voice. I asked Dr. Porter about it and he said the Health Insurance Portability and Accountability Act (HIPAA) prevented him from confirming any details about another family.

Either way, having Josh with me for Joe's delivery seemed impossible and bringing Cole with us was out of the question.

Chapter 23

Monday

I hadn't put the crib together. I was just so scared that I'd
have to take it apart. It was a gift when I was pregnant with
Cole. It had bite marks from the baby that everyone said was
too young to be getting teeth. Or standing up. One of the
sides got broken when *someone* tried to stretch their back
after a particularly long night of pacing the floors with a
teething 4-month-old. We couldn't afford a new crib so we
told the manufacturer the broken piece had come in the box
that way. We used it as a toddler bed for a while. It could
hold me and Cole if I curled up in a ball. Now it was all just
sitting against the wall, in pieces, waiting to be assembled
again.

I hadn't bought any clothes for the baby. I figured we could
rush out and get some if we had someone to wear them who
would actually come home.

Around 2:00 in the morning on the 12th I got up to go to the
bathroom. Not unusual for a six and a half month pregnant
lady. The house was silent. Josh and Cole were sound

asleep. I thought it was a good time to have a chat with the person in my belly. I wasn't in any pain or feeling any discomfort but I was feeling the anxiety creeping in. I took a deep breath and felt my feet on the cold floor and I asked Joe if he could hear me. We had decided to call our baby Joe. I didn't have any other names lined up for later babies, and I thought of saving the name. It occurred to me that this person I was growing was my child whether he did things his own way or the way we wanted him to. In fact he already sounded a lot like my great grandmother.

His second name was Grayson. I worried about a potentially stillborn baby being called Gray Son. Josh and I talked about stuff like that more often than you might imagine.

I asked Joe if he could forgive me. I told him I was sorry that I had been such a bad Mom so far and that I was done being scared of the tubes and surgeries and whatever squeamish tasks lay ahead. I was going to be the best Mom for him and I would fight for him and find doctors who would help him live and I would stop thinking about myself so much. His Dad and I and his big brother Cole were so happy he was in our life and he was already making our lives better just by being in it with us. And then I said the words I had heard in a class years before. Words that tell the universe to bring on the next phase of life whatever that may be. Words that trust in what the future holds and in our own ability to handle it. "I am here, I am open, I am ready."

I said them out loud and as I sat there with my belly in my hands, my son kicked and punched with both hands and both feet. It wasn't one punch or one kick - it happened all over my belly as though he had heard me and wanted me to know it would be okay no matter what happened. I went back to bed and fell asleep.

Chapter 24

Tuesday

When I got up in the morning I didn't feel so sick anymore. I told Josh we were going to Osh Kosh to buy some clothes for our new baby. He asked if I was sure and I told him that if we lost the baby, the least of my concerns would be a handful of clothes in the closet and if we had to return it, maybe that would just give me something to do. So we drove to Freeport like I had literally dozens of times when we were expecting Cole. I knew every inch of Carters and Osh Kosh and it was so wonderful to go in there with some hope in my back pocket.

I found matching sweaters for Cole and Joe. I bought the six month size against Josh's advice to buy the preemie stuff. I pointed out that if Joe was covered in tubes, he'd need sweaters we could take on and off easily and he wasn't going to spend his time in those hospital onesies. I stocked up on all the big brother shirts for Cole and bought some little matching splash pants for the two of them. You know the kind drug dealers still wear even though they haven't been popular since the eighties. I thought they'd look like little thugs and I loved it.

I would hold up the big and little size and ask Josh to imagine Cole holding his brother and how big he would look.

We went next door to Dunkin Donuts and celebrated with some hot chocolate and gross breakfast food. When we got home I hung up all the tiny and not so tiny clothes in the closet with ours.

Chapter 25

Wednesday

I woke up surprised that the good feeling was still around. I felt lighter. The nausea was gone and so was the anxiety. We went shopping again but this time in Portland at the Maine Mall. We went to Old Navy, my favourite store for maternity clothes, and then Cole wanted to go play in the little play area that had been set up by the Portland Jetport. I told them to go on ahead while I sat in the car because my phone was ringing with a Newfoundland number. At first I thought it was Revenue Canada or something so I pretended not to know who this Vickie person was that they were looking for. Turned out it was an old friend of ours who didn't know what had been going on with Joe.

I explained the diagnosis and how scared we had been but that we were feeling much better the past few days. Paul told me he had faith in us doing the right thing because we were good, loving people. I was confused by his words and I said well the crisis is sort of over, we've already decided to carry through with the pregnancy and take it as it comes and we're doing okay. He again said we were good people and he trusted we would do the right thing. I told him Joe had extra fingers and toes and that Josh and I had joked about what a good guitar player he would be. I was planning to make extra large mitts. He was basically a superhero.

Paul didn't laugh at the jokes. It was an odd conversation but he told me to call if there was any news or if there was any way he could help to just let him and his wife know. When I hung up, I still felt pretty good about where we were and what lay ahead.

On the way home, we went to Wendy's on Maine Mall Road. We decided to eat in the car since we were all crowded out. Out of nowhere I had this unbelievable urge to pee. It felt as if someone had fallen asleep and their elbow was digging straight into my bladder. It felt like dead weight. I was curled up in a ball in my seat trying to figure out how to get inside the restaurant without peeing in my pants. Josh started the car and drove around the building to get me closer and when I moved to get out, the urge passed as fast as it had hit. I finished my nuggets and even got a frosty and didn't give it a second thought.

Chapter 26

Thursday afternoon

When I got up in the morning on Valentine's Day I gave Harley a snuggle to say Happy Birthday and made some breakfast. Harley was a rescue dog who had been found wandering the main road in the Goulds back home. We had been looking for a dog for months and couldn't find one we connected with. Harley was no exception. She was barking and loud and obnoxious when we first saw her in the kennel outside the animal shelter. My brother happened to be with us that day and seemed drawn to her. When he reached through the fence she immediately dropped to the ground to have her belly scratched. I looked over at Josh and said "That's our dog."

I felt like she might be a kindred spirit. Hard to take at first and gave off all the wrong impressions but possibly not the worst dog ever.

The adoption was rough. The other dogs in the shelter had

parvo and were dying and they wouldn't let us take her home. We insisted that we loved her and if she died from parvo, we would make sure her last few days were comfortable. They insisted she had to stay and be observed for signs of the disease. We visited her every day for a week. Josh would sit at one end of the long hall and I'd be at the other saying "Go get Josh" and she'd bolt to him, fur rustling and tail wagging.

Then Josh would say "Go get Vickie" and she'd come bounding back to me.

When the week was up all the other dogs had been put down but our little fighter was doing great. She still had puppy teeth so they estimated she was about ten weeks old. When I counted back the weeks I saw a chance to give Valentine's Day a better connotation than the day I left my abusive first marriage and we declared that to be our dog's birthday.

On Harley's sixth ballpark anniversary of birth I was feeling pretty good and started the day with breakfast for all of us. Around lunchtime I got that dead weight feeling pushing on my bladder again and it dawned on me that the last time I felt Joe kick was a few nights ago in the bathroom when I had literally invited whatever was coming next.

I called Dr. Porter.

The drive over was a blur. I remember the wooden block game that Cole was playing with in the waiting room. All the little beads on bent wires and each side had a different brain buster challenge. The hum from the noise machine and the painting on the wall of a C-section that my OB/GYN had painted himself from one of his own deliveries. The large encasement display of all the babies he had delivered over the years - some with older siblings he had also delivered.

I walked down the familiar hallway and into a room that had become comfortable. I got up on the exam table and made some light jokes and watched Dr. Porter's face while he moved the Doppler around. He checked my belly for a solid twenty minutes trying to find the heartbeat. He looked me in the eye and ever so softly said "Victoria, I can't find Joe's heartbeat. Let's get you over to the hospital."

I sat up and he motioned for me to follow him down the hall to his office. I had never been past the examination rooms at his practice.

Josh and Cole came in behind us and we all sat down while he called Michele to book me for an urgent ultrasound. We sat there in silence for a moment after he hung up the phone.

"Can I ask before I lose my mind if it will be okay to try again for another baby?"

"How long do we need to wait?"

"Will they need to do an autopsy if Joe doesn't make it?"

"What are the options for burial and cremation?"

"Is there any chance he's in there?"

Michele buzzed back and said "They're waiting for Victoria over at Maternal Fetal Medicine. She needs to get over there right away."

Dr. Porter hugged me in the hallway. He promised he would go to the hospital if the news was bad. I stopped at the reception desk and made small talk with his wife Cathleen. She had an enormous bouquet of roses. She said oh yes Doug sends me roses every year for Valentine's Day. Michele firmly reminded me that they were waiting for me at the hospital. I said something about seeing them soon.

Josh went out to start the car and buckled Cole in and I stood on the sidewalk and called Gail. She was still at work and when she answered I said, "I know this is too much to ask a person on their birthday but can you come meet me at the hospital and can you bring your camera."

She was at MFM before we arrived. She didn't have time to get back home and get her own camera so she borrowed an identical camera from the police station that they use to photograph crime scenes.

I stayed calm. I didn't want to make anyone feel bad. I didn't want to rely on someone else to calm me down.

I don't know exactly when I planned on letting my guard down. I had my mind already set that I wasn't going to fall apart or be a slobbering mess in front of anyone. I would just get through it. I didn't really schedule any time for grief or pain or reality. I wanted it to be over if there was no hope and my punishment for such awful feelings was that I would keep a stiff upper lip and not allow myself to feel bad.

They brought me into the ultrasound room at the end of the hallway on the left. I ducked out to use the bathroom to smell that fucking soap one more time and look at the pictures of dilated cervixes on the wall. When I went back in the room, I sat on the crinkly white paper that covered the bed. The technician confirmed my name and date of birth and asked me to lay back. I know Josh and Cole and Gail were in the room but I have no idea where.

The technician put her hand on me as she reassured me it would just take another minute. She had to take a picture of

Joe's heart from every possible angle and there was just one more to go. She switched off the machine and started wiping my belly as she said how sorry she was. I asked her to check one more time. She agreed to check again but in that way you humour a person who has lost their mind. She squirted more gel on my belly and turned the machine back on and there was Joe – with his back facing us, cuddled into my midsection. I asked if his head was nestled in my right side and she said yes it is. He looked as if he had snuggled into me the way Cole did when he would fall asleep on me. Only Joe wasn't moving. His tiny chest wasn't moving up and down, his hands weren't reaching out in his sleep to make sure I was there…he was gone….just still in my belly.

I remember making some sort of moan type of screeching sound and it felt like every hand in the room reached out to comfort me. I didn't want to be touched. I wanted Joe to turn over and raise his little arm on the screen like he had during that first ultrasound when I was sure he wasn't growing in there. I wanted reassurance that everything was going to be okay and this was just a horrible, endless nightmare.

We moved our truck from MFM's parking lot because we couldn't leave it there overnight and drove across the street to Maine Medical Center. I had walked the same hallways from the parking garage to the Birth Center at MMC through five false alarms and one real one when I was pregnant with Cole but I didn't see a familiar tile on the floor, wall or ceiling as we went up to deliver Joe. I walked in the room they pointed me to and saw the bassinet that would hold my deceased child. I was so scared of labour when that glass cradle waited for Cole. So scared of the pain and worried that he might not be perfect and healthy and terrified in every cell that I couldn't get through it. None of that scared me this time around as much as the thought of how we were going to get my lifeless son from my belly to that tiny bed. It was like a small funeral home waiting to take him from me. No joy. No anticipation. No wondering how much he weighed or what his first cry would sound like.

It was around two in the afternoon. We had plans that day to go to Walmart to buy diapers for Cole. I wanted to go there first and buy a toothbrush and then go home and get a different jacket because the one I was wearing was not one you lose a baby in. Nobody would let me leave. They seemed to believe it was really about a goddamn toothbrush. They kept assuring me the hospital would give me one.

I was supposed to be induced. Some intern came in and said he was going to administer the medication that would get things underway and I said no, my own doctor is coming over and I don't want anyone else touching me. The medical team looked puzzled and said they would go call my doctor as he was likely unaware that I expected him to be there. I assured them he had promised me exactly that.

Four hours later Dr. Porter walked in and within seconds had the pill placed wherever it had to go. By then I had been admitted and had eight different puncture wounds from unsuccessful attempts to run an IV. I kept asking them to just forget it and they insisted it was procedure in case something went wrong. Eventually someone from emergency came and ran the line in about a minute.

The nurses thought I was a lot of fun. They were asking for my medical history and when I said my grandmother had a stroke a few years before she died they asked on what side. I said I think it was her right because she was right handed but I'm not sure. The room was silent for a long time and I said "Oh wow, did you mean what side of the family?"

Everyone burst out laughing and I asked if that would be the joke of the night on the labour and delivery floor and the nurse nodded, yes it absolutely would be. "Sorry to say but yes, that was hilarious."

Gail called her family who had planned a birthday dinner for her. She called Shelley, a friend of ours, and told her what was happening. Shelley asked if we needed anything. I said the only thing was an outfit for Joe to be cremated in and a bank account in his name so people could send donations for Cole in lieu of flowers. Shelley said she'd take care of it.

Induction is kind of a weird thing. They warned me that nothing might happen for a long time but then it would start almost out of nowhere and hit me like a freight train. I was supposed to stay laying down after the first dose but they had brought up a tray of cardboard for me to eat. I loved the food when I was there having Cole.

Four hours later Dr. Porter breezed through and administered another dose of the induction medication. Gail joked about how odd it was to see him and not have to get an internal exam. That was around ten o'clock. Again he warned me it might take a while.

I asked Gail to call Shelley and see if she was on her way over. Shelley had decided to wait until the morning to do the things she promised. It just felt like one more thing. Josh was driving around Portland letting a sleeping Cole get some rest when I called. I asked my husband to find some preemie pajamas to put on his second born so that Joe wouldn't be cremated in a hospital-issued onesie.

At eleven I started to feel some cramping. Gail called Josh

and told him it might be time. There was a lot more blood than I was comfortable with when I went to the bathroom so I got back in bed. The pain started to get worse. I buckled up on all fours and Gail would shove her fist into the end of my tailbone while the pain was intense. It's a sanity-saving technique for regular labours and hearse deliveries alike. You can also use a tennis ball instead of a fist but we didn't have one. Eventually Gail's arms were exhausted since no amount of pressure is too hard. Olivia Smith had taken over as my nurse. She didn't have any tennis balls to give us but she had rolled up a ball of medical tape for Gail to use.

Olivia had curled up in a chair in my room when her shift started and assured me she would stay for the duration. I apologized for ruining her Valentine's Day. She had just recently gotten married. She said I could ask her anything.

My first question was how she managed to handle these types of deliveries. She actually had volunteered for the shift when she found out there was a loss on the floor. A lot of the nurses had trouble with these cases and she believed if was she capable, then it was her duty or perhaps her gift to cover. She wondered if she could still do them if she ever had kids of her own.

My next question was whether she could take down the life-sized laminated photo of the healthy smiling baby that was on the closet door staring at me. It was just a poster for the hospital and you barely notice it when your own child looks like that - you know, pink and breathing. She ripped it down and shoved it in the closet.

We talked about offering a self-defense class for the female nurses who did night shifts.

I asked her if Joe would be cold when he came out. She said no not at first. He'll be normal body temperature but since he wasn't pumping blood through his body on his own, he would get cold rather quickly.

Close to midnight Josh got back with Cole. He had picked up diapers like our normal day should have gone and then he passed me a bag with a pair of preemie pajamas to send along with Joe's body to the funeral home.

I asked for medication for the pain.

The contractions hurt from my hips to my knees and I was trying to smile and talk through it to my friend, son and husband.

At about 12:45 in the morning I said something's happening, I can't get comfortable. Another nurse came in to help Olivia and started yelling at me that there was no way it was the baby and that I should lay down.

I pulled my pants off and got back on all fours. I laid on my elbows and rocked my hips back and forth to ease the pain. Olivia and Gail kept rubbing my back and Josh was standing by the door terrified. Gail asked him if he wanted to step in and he held up Cole's hand with a helpless look on his face. Gail bolted over and bent down to Cole's eye level and asked him if he wanted to go find some popsicles and there was such a relief that washed over me as Josh knelt in front of me and held both of my hands. He just kept saying "It's going to be okay, it's going to be okay."

I was crying and rocking back and forth and the second nurse went to check me and said "She's right, something's happening, get the doctor NOW." Olivia took her place and just barely caught Joe who had emerged inside an intact bag of waters at 12:50 am. There was no contraction, no cramp, no pain, just a warm sensation and then relief. Olivia told me to stay very still and the other nurse came back in to tell us the doctor was on his way. He pushed past her in the doorway and took Joe from Olivia's hands. They were all standing behind me. They let me get up and put on fresh pants after they removed the membrane. There was no afterbirth, no stitches, no need for any medical work at all. I stood up off the bed and let Josh hold me. It may have been a hard pregnancy but Joe was the most perfect, painless and fast delivery of all time.

A baby born in the caul was supposed to be a sign of good luck. I was afraid to look at him. Between the cleft palate and the omphalocele and the fact that he wasn't breathing, I expected him to look like a bag of ground beef with eyeballs that I couldn't be sure would even be closed. I asked how he looked.

Dr. Porter spoke first. He said "Victoria he's adorable. You have to see this. He's holding his little hands together like he's praying."

The blankets were up on the sides of the bassinet and I avoided looking in until I got right up to him. He was beautiful. And so peaceful. He was also a motley mix of dark blue and purple and deep gray. I wanted to hold him.

He was wrapped in a hospital blanket when they passed him to me. I immediately started unwrapping him and lifted my shirt to hold him against my belly. They recommend skin to skin for newborns because if baby is warm the mom's body will automatically cool down to lower his body temperature and if he's cold, mom will warm him up. It's a biological reaction. I remember tears dropping onto my shirt as I looked down at him. Everyone was afraid to move or say anything and I asked them all to leave.

I held Joe's body against me and I rocked and paced around the room and started singing California Dreamin' to him. It was Cole's favourite song when he was a baby and it made me feel like a mother whenever I sang to sooth my child. I got through the first verse and the chorus before I started to feel overwhelmed with disconnection. He was starting to cool down and I wanted him to meet his family.

I opened the two doors to the hallway and went out to find everybody. I had Joe wrapped back up in his blanket and I saw a laminated picture on my door. I realized that I was wandering the hall of labour and delivery holding my deceased baby around these rooms that were bringing new life into the world and I worried that we might scare one of the new moms if they were walking the halls having contractions, hopeful and anxious to meet their perfect babies.

Everyone came back in my room and I saw them closing the door behind them and pulling over the curtain for protection it seemed.

We took pictures of Dad holding Joe and of Cole sitting beside me while I held Joe. I wanted them to hold hands and we got one blurry shot but Cole wanted to pull away and I listened to that. I had read some things to do when a stillbirth is likely and I'm grateful for the stories like ours that people had shared. One piece of advice was to look for one good and perfect thing when my baby arrived. No matter what it is, you find one thing to focus on and you squeeze some joy out of that one detail.

It was Joe's thigh muscles. They looked like a miniature version of his father's legs. Cole's looked identical when he was born. Most of his other body parts looked like he had a chromosomal abnormality that would eventually make everything not work, but his little legs were so perfect.

The extra fingers and toes weren't as prominent as I expected. They weren't all full digits. The one on his left hand was more like a skin tag beside his pinky finger and in his little fist, he was almost holding it in the palm of his hand.

I chose that hand to get the picture I carry with me to this day everywhere I go. I wrapped Joe's fingers around my index finger and wrapped our hands in the hospital blanket so that's all you can see.

All of his fingers together made up the distance between the first and second knuckle of my finger. On the back of his hand, the skin had little pockets of gas and by the time we took the picture, the skin has peeled back to make a little heart shape. He was 1 pound and 11 ounces. He made it to 26 and a ½ weeks gestation.

Chapter 27

Thursday evening

I knew I could probably do a whole funeral service for Joe but I was afraid it would be just me, Josh and Cole sitting in an empty church. In lieu of a proper burial I asked for a priest to come in and bless Joe in our hospital room. It was someone I had never met but I felt comforted by the sight of the collar. I tried to imagine it was my high school principal sitting there beside me. He laid his hand on Joe and anointed him with oil and the sign of the cross. We said a prayer together. He too asked if I had any questions. I said actually I do, we are ah....and my voice broke.....we are cremating Joe. We aren't going to be staying in Maine and I don't want to bury him here and leave him behind. Is that going to be okay? I'm Catholic.

He said in the dark ages when the plague wiped out thousands of Christians, they had no other choice than to cremate people after they passed so as not to spread the disease. So yes, it had been acceptable for some time.

He could have said "Yes, my child, your baby's spirit is resting comfortable in the arms of our Heavenly Father so no matter what happens to his body here on Earth he will rest there in joyful hope of the return of our divine saviour and one day he will be reunited with you and his father and his brother and fear not, for he is a child of God and God would never let you down. Diliges dominum deum tuum. In nomine patris et filii et spiritus sancti."

But no. He instead talked about the diseased bodies being burned during the black plague so they didn't make anyone else sick.

Good chat.

Chapter 28

Thursday night

Josh took Cole home to get some sleep and Gail made a bed on the bench against the wall. I asked if I could keep Joe with me and nobody had a problem with it. I cuddled into him like I would any baby of mine and talked to Gail for a while before we decided to get some sleep. I kept drifting off with my hand on Joe and my cheek against his blanket and I would dream about my child falling or dying or being cold and I couldn't warm him up. I'd wake up to a start and look at my lifeless son beside me and settle back down but it just kept happening again and again. Sometimes when you dream it's a relief to wake up and see that the horror was just your imagination but there was no escaping the corpse in my bed. He was getting colder and colder and I didn't want to ever let him go and I knew on some level that what I was thinking might be a sign of a breakdown so I buzzed the nurse at 6 am and asked her to come take Joe from me. I kissed his head and held him close for another moment and handed him to her and asked if I could have some Ativan. Within a couple of minutes she filled my IV with the sweet release of narcotics that tried to help me forget where I was, who I was and what had just happened.

Chapter 29

Friday morning

Around 10 am a very large woman came in and said she was sorry for my loss and that there was a packet of information for mothers of lost babies that would be provided to me by the hospital before I left. She swished back out of the room. Then a nurse came in with my discharge papers that said if I experienced a high fever, bleeding or any other unusual symptoms to call the hospital right away.

From there we drove to the funeral home. It was the one the police used when they found bodies and that's why it was recommended to us - nobody really has a favourite.

I met a young man who had just started working there and brought us through a room with small caskets and then to a table in the lobby area where he handed me some brand new catalogues of urns and cremains jewelry and fingerprint necklaces and lamps.

I assumed they would give you something to take everything

home after it was all done but he pushed us to order an urn. I saw one with a clover on it that spoke to me and said here this one and gave him back the catalogue. He wanted to know details like if we wanted to be there while it was being done and I said absolutely not. I don't want to know it's happening. Please just call us when it's over. Oh well some families....yeah I don't care. I don't feel very good about cremating my baby so please don't tell me any details. There's an outfit we'd like put on him and we don't want to know anything until it's over. That was Friday morning.

Chapter 30

Journal - February 16, 2013

I can't breathe. I can't sit still. I keep picturing Joe on a cold metal table in the morgue laying there naked. I feel like I've betrayed him. I want to go pick him up and call it all off and bring him home. The cremation is supposed to happen sometime today. The phone rings and it's the funeral home. Thank God it's over. No, they want to know for sure what font we want them to use on the urn we ordered. Is the cremation done yet? No, there was a mixup at the hospital. It won't be done until tomorrow.

Chapter 31

I don't know where we went that day I just remember I had to get out of the house. And I can still see the door knob when we came home. It had a Sorry We Missed You, Please Call to Schedule ReDelivery doorknocker hanging from it. It was from a florist. Josh was bringing Cole in from the car so he pulled up the rear and asked what was wrong. I held up the card and asked if he had sent me flowers. Once when we had only known each other a couple of weeks he had sent flowers while he was still in North Carolina. They were beautiful and I still have the card that was attached. It took a little while to tell him that while appreciated, I didn't enjoy watching them die or having to throw them out. Call it OCD or whatever, but I despise flowers.

I had expressed the exact concerns when Josh and I got married. His mother had flown up to attend the ceremony and wanted to know if I had anyone taking care of the flowers. She was staying with us in another tiny apartment and wanted to make the most of the trip so had booked a few days before and after our wedding. The house felt full so I pushed in a direction nobody expected and invited my 2 nieces and 2 nephews and my little brother to spend the night. I knew they liked me. They were happy in sleeping bags on the floor and we made a whole thing of it. They came to the play I was in that evening at the LSPU Hall where their new uncle Josh was also helping out as part of the backstage crew and afterwards we came home and made cheese dip and rice krispie treats and giggled until the wee hours of the morning. My youngest niece said she didn't want to make the cookies but we figured out she just didn't want to get her hair sticky so I let her borrow a ponytail holder. It was a pretty memorable night.

The morning of the wedding a knock came on the door and someone ran to answer it. A delivery driver was standing there holding three dozen red and pink carnations. Granted that was the flower I had mentioned a preference for but in the same breath I had also said please send them to my funeral as I don't want them when I'm alive. My oldest niece took the delivery and turned to me kind of dumbfounded and not sure what to say. My mother-in-law came rushing out the hallway and said "Oh they're here! You can't have a wedding without flowers, it's just not riiiiiiiiiiight!"

Five years later my husband was standing in front of me with the same dumbfounded look on his face. It was a mix of rage and embarrassment that he couldn't stop what was happening and whatever else a father feels when he is grieving and trying to mop his wife up off the doorstep. I took Cole's hand and went inside and asked Josh to refuse the delivery. I didn't care how much it cost or who they were from. I overheard him a while later on the phone. He was yelling and asking whoever had sent the flowers if they were trying to push me all the way over the edge.

Chapter 32

Journal - February 17, 2013

I'm in hell. Surely this is just punishment for allowing a cremation at all. Would an empty funeral be worse than this? I cannot bury Joe here because I've grown to hate this fucking place with a burning passion. If I ever get out of here, I'm never coming back.

The funeral home called. Josh answered the phone while I picked up Cole to hold him close. I overheard him answering questions about the urn. You have GOT to be kidding me.

Chapter 33

Josh came straight over to hug me when he got off the phone with the funeral home. He wasn't doing any better than I was. We still had to eat and bathe and take care of Cole. We just wanted this nightmare to be over so we could be here together and begin grieving. We couldn't do that while Joe was still out there somewhere. We didn't even know where he was at that point because there was a 'mixup at the hospital.' I put his name Joe Grayson Morgan on the death certificate but the hospital labels a baby by the mother's last name which was Linegar. Rather than call me or involve me in any way, they held Joe's body for two extra days.

We drove somewhere in South Portland that day and I remember the combination of hormones and shock and disappointment and uneasiness of what we were doing with Joe's body and as we crossed the bridge that overlooks the other hospital in Portland, I found myself daydreaming about how this may have gone had I delivered at the Catholic hospital. Maybe Joe wouldn't be laying on the cold metal table with the absolute unthinkable about to be done to him. I mean I could see him lying there. Maybe I nodded off but I know I felt his presence. And then I saw Joe. Not the helpless lifeless hopeless body that I had said goodbye to just a few days earlier but a bigger person with straight dark hair. He was older and looked a little like my youngest nephew. He let me know that the tiny broken body at the hospital hadn't been him for quite some time and this was not going to hurt him in any way. It was simply the best we could do right now and he was not in pain.

I had cold tears on my cheeks when I felt him not with me anymore. When we got to Sam's Club I waited in the car while Josh and Cole ran inside and I called a friend who had lost her grown child. I've heard people come into your life for a reason, a season or a lifetime. That day as I sat in the front seat of our truck asking Lois if she thought I was crazy and describing how my dead son had somehow spoken to me without words, she relayed her own story to me. Her daughter was in an urn on a shelf in her home and she might never bury her. But there was no doubt that her daughter had communicated with her after she died and it was something only a parent who has been there would ever understand.

Oh and my milk came in today. Nobody warned me that my body still thinks there's a baby so I can't cross my arms and I'm swollen well up into my neck. I'm almost glad for the pain.

Chapter 34

February 18, 2013

Funeral home on the phone first thing this morning. Surely it's done now and you guys are done torturing me right? No sir, please let your wife know that it will be done later today, we just had one more question about the urn you ordered.

I called them back myself. I was concerned about how such incompetent morons might be handling my son's body. If they would even bother to put the clothes on him that we had provided. And why they would give me the most inexperienced funeral director in the organization as this was definitely not a cookie cutter scenario. I screamed, I swore, I cried, I demanded an apology. I demanded an explanation of why they were charging us $500 for a service that was supposed to be free for stillborn babies. I threatened to tell the Portland Police Department how horrifically unprofessional they were so they'd stop sending business their way.

There was an extensive apology and a reversal of the cremation fees and I was still what one might call hysterical. I told them to cancel the urn too. New Guy the Undertaker had already told me it was impossible because it was engraved and I told this idiot on the phone that we had walked through a room of engraved urns and they could just use it for a show piece. I don't want anything from them to ever be in my home. The abject horror I feel that they still have my son's body is a feeling they haven't invented harsh enough words for yet.

Once again the funeral director tells me the cremation will take place later this afternoon and that we will be notified when we can come pick up our son. He assured me there would be no more calls until the procedure is complete. I hope he doesn't call back ever again.

Chapter 35

Joe was finally cremated six days after we lost him. Six days. We had to wait a while before we could go pick him up because his ashes needed time to cool. What a fucking sentence that is.

My therapist wanted me to get back to regular life as soon as possible. I wasn't actually getting out of bed but Cole was waking up each morning and pulling me by the hand into the day. He kept talking to my belly saying hi to his brother and trying to give him high fives. I was crying so often and he would run and get a box of tissues and wipe my face every time he saw it. I felt like I was ruining his life.

I went back to school. I had an exam to write in the eyeball class and my professor still hadn't responded to my email. Sitting in the desk was much easier without the big belly. The words on the page went blurry and I wondered if anyone saw me there sobbing.

I went to a grief support group at the hospital. The lady who runs it lost a child 40 years ago and she told us that in all that time, the number of babies lost each year for all the same reasons has not changed. The other stories were heartbreaking. I was the only one there on my own. Some of the others had kids at home but they also had babysitters so their partners could attend and share too.

It was only 15 minutes away from our house and on the way home I had my first urge to drive into the wall of rocks on the side of the highway.

Chapter 36

Trisomy 13 is said to occur in 1 in 10,000 babies. How many of them are terminated as soon as the diagnosis is received is unknown but the rate of divorce among couples who have a stillbirth is 40 percent higher than those who have not suffered a loss. That was the topic of discussion at my second week in grief support. I was there alone, again.

I knew there was no chance of meeting someone that could ever take me away from Josh. I wasn't in great shape mentally but I was going to therapy twice a week and I was journaling and writing a blog and talking about my loss in a support group.

I had not considered a scenario where someone who had previously broken my heart might come back into my life.

I was married once before. It was a terribly abusive relationship and I tried leaving numerous times before I finally got up the courage to get out all the way. For a little while I lived in my car and camped on friend's couches. But I got out. And when I was newly single and high on life I had a friend who had recently broken up with his wife. He was from the mainland and working in Newfoundland and I was crazy about him. It didn't last long before long he finished his contract and reconciled with his wife but not before he gutted me.

Ten years later I was living in Maine married with a child and saw a newspaper article about a Canadian who now lived about ten minutes away from me in Freeport. I sent him an email to welcome his family to Maine and he wrote back right away inviting me to text instead and gave me his cell number. I told Josh about the correspondence and he looked at me like he was afraid I was going crazy.

My therapist was okay with it. In fact he was almost excited to hear the updates. At first he'd call him by name and eventually he just had a nickname for the guy and would start our sessions with "Have you heard from T-Squared lately (Initials T.T.)?"

It was the wedge I didn't need in my relationship that's for sure. I started really resenting Josh. And here I had this old friend who was so comforting and said all the right things. I knew I was risking my marriage and the opportunity to raise our son together but I started to blame Josh for losing Joe. If

I had just married someone else then maybe this never would have happened. It was easier than blaming my advanced maternal age and trauma history and a million other factors that have never been proven to cause chromosomal abnormalities.

I had another friend at the time that I was confiding in and told her all about the texts and emails from my former boyfriend who lived just up the road. It was a wonderful distraction from what was actually happening to me. She was fully supportive of a fling.

It didn't take long at all for the opportunity. My old flame started telling me he was having marital trouble and wanted to see me. I went in our spare bedroom to text him back when Josh came upstairs and opened the door to check on me. He was worried. And he wasn't comfortable with how secretive I was being all of a sudden.

I never told Josh that this guy was telling me that he could never forget me and how amazing I was. I've found that no matter what is missing in your life there is always going to be someone who will come along and provide that exact thing. It wasn't Josh's fault that we didn't have time together to talk or grieve. It wasn't his fault that there was deafening silence from nearly all of our family after we lost our baby. I felt forgotten. And this guy remembered me. I knew I was a piece of shit for even entertaining the idea. I just wanted to stop hurting.

I often wondered why everybody trusted me to do the right thing or at least not do the wrong thing with T-Squared. Nobody was concerned that I was going to run away or leave my family but I didn't have much confidence at all. And I wasn't interested in a fling. I wanted an escape. A new life. This guy was offering texts behind his wife's back. I kept telling him my husband was amazing and we should all meet someday. Sometimes I even talked about Joe. The texts slowed significantly.

I left the house one night with full intention to go wait for him somewhere. I had a cd of cheating country songs that I listened to again and again and on the dashboard was a picture of Cole. I had put it there to remind myself to not drive into oncoming traffic. He texted something flirty and I texted back "I bet you say that to all the girls."

What happened after my sardonic text that night was a blur of rage and tears. He started sending me angry texts and I saw a glimpse of his drunken Irish temper that scared the bejeezus out of me. I had stopped at Walmart and was walking around crying and sending apologies over and over.

I didn't think I could handle losing someone else.

When I went back to my car I sat in the dark for a long time. I can't say that I saw Joe's face but I felt him with me that night. This wasn't how he wanted things to turn out. He didn't want me to leave his Dad or end up sharing custody of his brother. This was all just so wrong.

I turned off the sad music and drove home and helped with Cole's bath. After he went to bed I texted my suitor and asked him if he knew he had broken my heart a decade before. That I was a wreck when he left Newfoundland without a word and that I was not in a good place since I had lost a baby. He claimed he had no idea.

I stopped responding to his messages. Had he pushed more I can't say what would have happened although I'd like to say my self-respect would have kept us apart.

About a year later I saw his picture in the paper again. After he wasn't in my life anymore he took up with an underaged girl and the court report said it started over texts. It crossed my mind that the police must have wondered who I was when they saw texts from me on his phone. My therapist laughed when I mentioned my concern. He pointed out I was in no way a victim in that story. I found it funny that he thought that was what I was going for.

As humiliating as this part of my journey is for me, I thought it unfair to leave it out. I kind of laughed at the statistics about couples who break up after a loss. I was married to my best friend. I was pretty certain nothing could come between us but I grossly underestimated grief. I still believe Joe sent me that distraction to keep my tires on the pavement until I found my way back to Josh and Cole.

Chapter 37

Journal - March 20, 2013

Joe has been gone a month and five days. By now the hormones that follow delivery have settled down and I'm left with just me. No bulging belly. No kicks in the middle of the night. Cole doesn't wake up and kiss my belly and say good morning to his brother anymore. It's been a lifetime ago since we bought matching sweatshirts for them to wear in the pictures I imagined in spite of Joe's diagnosis.

I've looked through all the pictures and cried into the blankets we took from the hospital that covered his tiny body. I have a small box that contains his ashes and an ornament someone sent me this week. It's of a little boy holding his baby brother while they rock together in a rocking chair. I thought of smashing it into a million pieces. How could someone be so cruel as to send something that will never be possible in my life. Until I realized it was the only gift anyone had given Joe.

I threw out the milk samples that came in the mail to welcome my new baby. I got a letter from a doctor in North Carolina. My mother-in-law had emailed asking random surgeons if any of them would operate on Joe while I was still carrying him.

My breast milk was now dried up and my cycle had restarted and physically, things are back to normal.

"It's all part of God's plan." Someone actually said that to me. I wanted to slam my forehead off the wall. No, I don't think God was up there above us all taking our babies. No not everything happens for a reason. Some things just suck. I wish there was someone or something at times like this who would hold us in the crook of its arm and helps us breathe when it becomes too painful to do it for ourselves.

I can't believe it's snowing again. I kept promising myself that we would get through this winter. I don't feel like I'm ever going to be whole again. We've talked about having another baby someday but there is no way I could ever fill that void in my brain where my son should be. And not even the knowledge of how sick he would have been and all the interventions he would have needed just to breathe and eat changes the devastation I feel. He should have been healthy. He should be still growing in my uterus. I should be still pregnant complaining about how much my skin is stretching and reading books about sibling rivalry.

It's almost five in the morning. I'm out of words. The blue light will be coming in through the curtains pretty soon and life will start again. Whoever said 'one day at a time' was awfully optimistic. I'm counting breaths. I have a son and husband who need me. How do people do this without someone to pull them out of bed each day?

Chapter 38

Journal - April 2, 2013

Joe was stillborn a little over six weeks ago. I am not equipped to deal with losing a baby. A child. A person whose every cell came from my own body save for one.

I can't remember how pregnant I should be. I try to do the math and my brain stops working. I just know I should be pregnant and something is terribly, terribly wrong.

I have learned a lot from Joe. I've had things cross my mind that I never dreamed I could consider. I understand suicide more now. I don't mean the pity-seeking, attention-grabbing attempts at suicide. I mean the deliberate, gun in the mouth, drive off a cliff, no turning back suicides. Maybe it isn't selfishness that drives people to suicide like I once believed. Perhaps sometimes it's the only way to stop the pain.

I've been having panic attacks again. Trouble sleeping, trouble eating. All the stuff I had gotten a handle on and they are back with a vengeance. The good news is that I am an old pro at battling depression. In a way, maybe being a survivor long before I ever got pregnant has prepared me for this.

I have to admit – I thought I had done my time. I really believed my life had turned around for the better and it would be mostly smooth sailing. Through the entire pregnancy I felt like this was happening to someone else. That when the time came, I would have a miracle baby who beat the odds and wouldn't have any of the problems the doctors were sure he would have.

Life just keeps on trucking. Doesn't matter how I feel or how bad I want things to slow down so I can catch my breath. The advice I keep getting is 'do the work' and 'sit with the grief.' It's as if they don't know I'm already carrying it around with me everywhere I go. I can't outrun it. I can only try to run with it strapped to my back. This is who I am now. A mother of two who only kisses one of them goodnight.

Yes I am very grateful for Cole but that guilt-laced approach of telling me how worse other people have it or be thankful for what you have – does nothing for grief. It doesn't make Joe any less gone.

I have given myself permission to be impatient, bitchy, standoffish, unreliable, late, emotional, irrational, needy,

clingy, ridiculous, irresponsible, impulsive, weepy, sad,
infuriated, suspicious, contemplative, sleepy, high, drunk,
repulsed, cold, bitter, annoying, obsessive, tactile, spacey,
jealous, vengeful...and that's all before second breakfast.

I get the feeling that's been the key to healing all this time.
Taking care of myself first. Honouring my feelings even if
they're ugly. If that's what I'm supposed to learn from all
this, great, I'm done. I'd like my son back now please.

Chapter 39

April 17, 2013

Joe has been gone for two months and two days. Whoever said time heals all wounds didn't have a fucking clue and certainly never lost a child.

If it's not obvious already, I'm still at 'angry' on the Kubler-Ross model for stages of grief. I'm teetering on the edge of depression but my anger keeps me from going over the edge and I'm living my life for spite at this point.

One of the hardest parts of this has been all the other losses that I am reminded of in our time of need. I imagine it's a lot like the way comfort food reminds you of good, contented times. Grief has a way of reminding me how bad I have felt in the past. There are some huge voids in my life and it's easier to focus my energy on those who are living because ultimately, I can't get mad at Joe for leaving.

A few days ago my husband and I were driving home from the park with a sleeping little boy in the back seat and we heard the news about the bombing in Boston. Back home the thought has always been that the U.S. is one big neighborhood and anyone who lives there must be just down the road from each other. And yet the phone never rang. Nobody emailed. Nobody texted. Don't worry. We're fine. Thanks for wondering. And then I remind myself that if Joe's death didn't warrant reaching out, it's delusional to think a bomb in Boston would trigger any emotion.

I read a blog post a couple of weeks ago from a man who had lost a child and he spoke about the dysfunction he had grown up with being even more apparent in his time of need. I felt like yelling at the computer screen I KNOW!

This has been the absolute loneliest time of my life. I wouldn't wish this on my worst enemy.

And though I walk through the valley of the shadow of death....

Chapter 40

I met a woman in the park who had a little boy about Cole's age and they both had out of control, curly blond hair. She was carrying her six-month-old son in her arms. She told me how jealous her first son was when his brother arrived. She said it was hell to see how angry he was. Then she added, actually it was heartbreaking.

Her kids were the same ages mine would have been apart. Yeah, heartbreaking came to mind for me too.

There are no words that take away the pain. The loss compounded with the loss of the friendships I thought I had really starts to feel like I am never going to recover. You waste so much time wondering what the hell is wrong with the world and lashing out and taking it out on those who are there – and it's all to avoid feeling what is really wrong in your life…that you have to go on without someone who you planned to have in your life forever.

I keep promising myself that although I might not be able to fight right now I am taking names and people better look out when I get back on my feet. It's a load of shit. I'm not going to be closed off from the world because of losing Joe. My life is already opening up to people I never would have met if not for him. I swear he is looking out for me and making sure I take care of myself and his brother and his dad. We are still a family. He has made my life so much more meaningful and that is precisely why it's so hard to not have him here. Imagine what he would have done with more time.

Chapter 41

Journal - May 2, 2013

Joe has been gone for eleven weeks. Twenty-two days from now would have been my due date. But instead of a ripe, swollen belly I have the tiniest paunch where my baby used to be and an emptiness that will not go away.

I don't have as much energy to be angry lately. If you've ever watched a NASCAR race there are certain tracks where the cars have steel plates placed somewhere on the engines to make sure they don't go above a certain speed. It's called restrictor plate racing. I'm living a restrictor plate life right now. I'm as happy and content with my life as a person who held her dead child's hand ten weeks ago can expect to be. I have many things in my life that I love and am grateful for and also this crushing weight on my entire body that feels bolted to me.

As the weeks pass, I feel less detached from Joe. I am becoming more comfortable when asked to say I have two children. When I was pregnant, there was a sort of surrealism – as though my mind hadn't fully gotten used to the idea of a new baby in my life. I wasn't one of those moms who fell instantly in love when I saw the positive pregnancy test. I knew the work that lay ahead and I tried to prepare for what would happen to my body. Since giving birth to Joe and touching him and holding him and carrying his ashes home, I am now free to love him and have a relationship with him – even if it is only in dreams and moments I think he has arranged for me.

The night we picked up Joe from the funeral home, it felt like there might be video cameras in the back of our truck filming my every move, watching for my reaction, some emotion but there was none. The tiny box was so much smaller than I expected and I did not feel the peace I expected when the funeral director handed it to me. I couldn't face going home so we stopped at the mall.

As we parked, I noticed the temperature reading on the dashboard. It was well below freezing. I couldn't leave Joe in the truck. I couldn't take him in the mall. My husband froze – not knowing what the right thing to say to his wife might be. Cole was already out of his car seat and had no idea why I wasn't moving.

The box was too big for my pocket. If I put the remains of my child in the diaper bag, the box would not be upright and I didn't want to upset his ashes. I just could not leave Joe in the car in the cold by himself. I had already left him behind at the hospital and allowed the funeral home to take him to be cremated. I could not let him down again.

It felt like we stood there for a long time before I finally decided, I need to take my sons into the mall with me. It may be the only time we ever get to go out as a family because God knows, I won't be removing Joe's ashes from the house once we bring him home. That would be crazy. Even in my shell-shocked state, I knew I couldn't start carrying this box everywhere I went even though I wanted to make jewelry out of it and never take it off. Ever.

Dark humor has become a normal part of our lives now. As we walked into the mall I said well at least I don't have to worry about the police report we would have had to fill out if someone had broken into the truck. "Officer, my son has been taken." "But ma'am your son is holding your hand. We only see one car seat." "Oh no I mean my other son. Someone stole my other son. He was in the truck by himself. Someone must have mistaken his box for..."

We laughed in that way bereaved parents do – is it okay for us to find that funny? Should we be laughing at anything right now? Can't we just enjoy a moment together anymore?

As we wandered through the people who had multiple children, I wondered if anyone could tell the diaper bag on my shoulder had extra wipes, three diapers, a plastic remote and Joe. I asked Josh if he thought we had ever walked by people who brought dead family members to the mall with them for the same reason and he said well you look like everybody else right now so maybe we did and just didn't know. Maybe we had walked by people before who were in this same hellish grief and we didn't even realize how painful it must have been to see our healthy little boy with us. How many women were holding their empty bellies when they saw mine so swollen and healthy with Joe just a week before. So much grief and sadness and pain and we were just wading through, unaware. Except now we know.

Honouring the fact that Joe was here and real and died has been a struggle for me. The silence surrounding the fact that I lost a child just added to the pain. It felt like people didn't consider it that big of a deal because he died before he was born. He wasn't full term. He would have been so sick anyway. It's not like we watched him die.

Every day when I log in to Facebook there is a new post

from Still Standing magazine. Each post is different but there is always an element of yeah, I get that, to every story. Moms (and Dads) who had babies die pre-term, at birth, at one year, two years, twenty years or younger than Joe don't diminish the grief my family is going through. They just share the pain. And how they got through it. This whole world I was oblivious to and now it's a part of my daily life.

I remember that old saying about be careful what you wish/pray for. Like if you ask for strength you don't get it but you get things that will make you stronger. HA! Too funny. Seriously, too funny.

Chapter 42

May 8, 2013

After my divorce went through in 2004, I took anti-depressants for a while. My doctor had suggested them a few times and I kept refusing but eventually I went in and said okay, Doc, I need help. I was a wreck. Back then I worried that the pills would kill any creativity I might have. They did. I worried they would numb me. They did. I worried they would be hard to live without. They were. I worried they would change my brain chemistry. I can't prove that last one but I know it took two solid years to feel like myself again.

I tried Celexa – the safest drug at the time for anyone who might get pregnant (in other words, not a nun). When I went to the doctor with a suspected pregnancy, he warned me to come back right away if I was expecting because he wanted me off those pills immediately. He said there were new studies saying perhaps they weren't as safe as previously believed. Trials can't be done on pregnant women so the findings have to be done after the fact. The results were in.

Luckily I wasn't pregnant at the time so I weaned off them (very slowly and with doctor's supervision) and haven't considered taking anything since.

Until yesterday.

I have all the same concerns as before except the root of my symptoms is drastically different. Years ago I was battling OCD, struggling to pay living expenses, flunking out of school, was estranged from my family and didn't have a whole lot to live for.

Yesterday I was supposed to be 37 weeks pregnant. Even though my son had numerous congenital malformations and problems with almost every organ and system – his death has affected me just as much as that of a healthy baby would have. I'm sad and angry but that seems pretty normal to me. It's only been three months. I haven't even reached my due date yet. Mother's Day is this weekend. It's kind of a rough time.

I explained all that to a nurse practitioner who tried to convince me she was the same as a psychiatrist. She is not a psychiatrist. She might have a prescription pad with her name on it, but she is not a doctor. She is not an MD. She is not even a licensed therapist. But her mind was set on me leaving there with a prescription for Zoloft. I even went as far as saying I would consider Celexa again since it had technically worked in the past. She said that was her second choice and pushed the Zoloft.

The days of trusting that every health professional I meet is going to have my best interests at heart or that they are even listening to me are gone. I was reminded of the cardiologist who told me he wouldn't recommend or encourage the surgery Joe needed on his heart because he wasn't worth saving. I had a feeling in the pit of my stomach that day and again yesterday.

I referred to the death of my son as the reason I was sitting in her office. I explained that he had a rare genetic disorder and died at twenty-six and a half weeks gestation. She replied "So you mean he was stillborn."

She asked me if I thought about hurting myself. Yes, every fucking day. It would be a way out of this pain. But I have a son and husband who need me who bring such joy to my life I can barely stand it. So I have many reasons to live, I just sometimes want to die when it hurts too much.

"Well that's not normal," was her reply. I kid you not. I looked at the floor to try and go to a happy place and block

out what she had said. So she bent her little squirrel head around to force me to make eye contact and told me two more times, "That's not normal."

She kept asking me if I thought about hurting my son or husband. No, of course not. She said no fantasies of killing them so you could all be a happy family. Nope. It's never crossed your mind? For the last fucking time, I don't think about hurting anyone but myself but you are coming dangerously close.

Obviously I didn't say that last part because I figured she might try to take my dog too.

I left her office feeling like someone had violated me. She balled my life up and told me in no uncertain terms that I was unstable and had to start thinking of my family and what they needed and I was no good to them the way I was.

This is day 82 of my journey as a bereaved mother. If you count the days since I found out Joe would likely die, it's been 130. When the first doctor delicately hinted that I should have expected this because of my advanced age (35). It was the first time I was told Joe didn't matter.

I have been through something difficult.

I am in no way saying medication is not a good fix for some people. But I am functioning. I am enjoying life with my son, husband and dog. I am going to therapy. I go to a support group. I am what they call 'doing the work.'

You know what would have been nice? If she had started the session with "I'm sorry for your loss. I have kids. I don't know what I would do if anything happened to them."

Instead she tore me down more than anyone has in a very long time.

Think someone will give you a break after you lose a child? Some people will. Some people on the other hand will not. She hid behind her clipboard and ignored all my questions. I want to have more children. She can't tell me a medication that crosses the placenta and comes out in breast milk will not affect a baby's brain chemistry. When I asked how kids turn out she said there wasn't enough evidence to say – we'd probably find out someday and know in hindsight what it caused.

I get out of bed every morning and try to live up to as many obligations as possible - with my family, with school, with teaching self-defense, with general upkeep of friendships. I am healing. I am going to trust that my body is telling me something every time I have a panic attack. That's not something to ignore.

This might take a very long time to go away. What I need is coping mechanisms. I have a worry stone someone gave me that helps if I rub it between my thumb and forefinger when the anxiety hits. It helps if I deal with the little obstacles life throws my way even if it means I may act a little inappropriately. I want to feel some of the pain. It keeps me connected to Joe. The day it stops hurting, I would worry that depression had taken me over and maybe I need some pills. As long as I'm hurting, I know I'm still alive.

It breaks my heart to see Cole run for tissues when he sees me crying. I explain to him that I'm sad about his brother. I think this is a normal part of life. We did after all lose a child. It would be abnormal at this point if I didn't cry. If I didn't feel anxious. And if I didn't feel outraged at someone who tells me I have a chemical imbalance and owe it to my family to take Zoloft.

I have to wonder sometimes if there are really people who nothing bad ever happens to. If they will just continue to be uncaring pricks for their whole life. It wouldn't change any of the things in my life so I guess it doesn't matter. I just wonder is all.

Chapter 43

Journal - May 14, 2013

We went to the zoo in Boston for Mother's Day. It was a tradition we started when I was pregnant with Cole. Moms get in for free. I figured Joe would have wanted us to do something special that maybe we could not have done had he survived. Perhaps that's the wrong way to look at it but that's how I got through the day. Joe would have been very, very sick and we would not have brought him home from the hospital. My partner and I would have been trading off time to be at the NICU and taking care of Cole. There would not have been trips to the zoo two hours away - especially if we had met Joe and had to watch him die. I barely made it through his stillbirth. So my gift to Joe and to Cole was to do something special with our time together. We had lunch at the cafe in the zoo. They have the greatest chicken strips and overpriced ice cream. It was called Joe's Safari Cafe.

I expected seeing the other families with multiple children would do me in but I stayed focused on us and took lots of pictures and listened to Cole's attempts at saying all the animal names. He's talking a lot these days and we are teaching him sign language. He spreads his arms real wide and says "This much" when I ask him how much we love his brother Joe. He gets it.

We had a call from a florist in Portland. He had an order come in and wanted to give me a heads up that I was the recipient. A lady had called in asked if she could tell the flower shop owner a story. Thinking it was a solicitation call, he hung up. Mother's Day is a very busy time for florists and he didn't have time for nonsense. She called back and started in again to the same response. When she called a third time and started cursing him out for being rude to a grieving woman, he hung up again. After talking it over with his business partner he called back to the originating phone number to see if it was a business number or a private citizen who had been calling. It was my mother-in-law. She wanted to send flowers to her daughter-in-law again but this time with a card that read "Happy Mother's Day. With Love, Joe."

The shop owner explained that there were stalker laws in Maine that prohibited him from doing that. And since he remembered feeling like garbage for attempting to deliver the flowers she had ordered when Joe died, he felt it was his duty to let me know she was trying to send more of the thing I hated to my house. I asked him to donate the delivery to anyone else who might like it. He offered to let me come pick out an Oxalis plant as that was something that would keep living and had also become somewhat of a symbol of Joe. I was too afraid the plant would die too so I never got around to picking up a plant from his flower shop.

I posted on Facebook that day that if anyone else thought of sending flowers with my dead son's name on them to please refrain. My friends responded with just the right amount of horror. My favourite was this one. Jessie was another bereaved mother from the support group and had posted a lengthy properly disgusted response to my complaint.

Jessie wrote: "People just don't fucking get it sometimes!!!!! Your heart and soul are broken and yes, your life is continuing without Joe - I mean what fucking choice do we have, right, but to shove your pain down your throat with flowers from him?? I just don't understand the logic behind that!! I so wish I would have been awake when you called last night because I'd really like to know the name of this person who thought this would be a good idea for you... From one grieving Mama to another, Hold Me Back!!!!!! I probably would have called the person and went into great detail about the impossibility that my son could have sent them but I'm pretty amped about Mother's Day myself. I've had so many people tell me to just be happy because I have two beautiful children here who want to celebrate me. Of course I'm going to let my other children celebrate me! But a part of my heart and soul is missing... I just want to say how about I cut off your arms and then tell you to be thankful you still have your legs... People can be such jerks! Even if their intention was in the right place on their end they can't even imagine what we are feeling. I can imagine you're feeling even more amped because your due date is coming up... Do what you need to do, do what's best for you and Cole & Joe! So much love and strength being sent your way from me. I'm here for you!!!! Xoxoxo"

There were so many others who rallied around me and sent love and healing and prayers but my mother-in-law replied directly to Jessie.

"My name is Mary Ann Sawyer. I am Joe's Grandmother. I sent flowers to several WONDERFUL mothers for mother's day - including my daughter in law. Since Joe is a daily part of Vickie's life and he IS my grandson, I wanted to remind her that she is a WONDERFUL mother to him - as well as Cole. There was no way for me to know she couldn't stand flowers. And I have apologized profusely. Jessie, if you'd like to private message me, I'd love to give you my number and we could discuss this further."

There were a host of responses directly to me after that from concerned friends who feared for my mental health and rage capacity after reading the exchanges that were being passed around. I posted a thank you for the support and reassured my social network that I was hanging in by a thread. One lady who has never said an undignified word in her life chimed in and said "Vickie, you may want to delete these posts for your sanity my friend. Love always. xo"

That seemed to piss my mother-in-law off even more. I guess there wasn't room on the card for these sentiments.

"I assure you all that I am VERY sorry for the horror and devastation my son and daughter in law have and continue to endure. I will never know the the abyss they are living in. I also assure you all that you do NOT have the whole story of the support I have tried to and continue to try to offer. So, judge away. We shall see how long Vickie leaves MY comments on line. She generally deletes them. I am not the one who started this public "pissing contest". Please don't misquote me. And, I have NEVER asked YOU for anything."

That last part wasn't exactly true. She did ask something of me. The week we lost Joe she wanted to come visit and be near Josh and Cole. I told her I needed time and she got very angry. I told her she could come up for our Mother's Day tradition instead and come to the zoo in Boston with us. She said she'd prefer to come up right away during our time of need. I insisted we needed some time alone and asked her to be a part of happy memories with her grandson instead of this dark, very personal, very private time. Grief was teaching me how to set boundaries and protect my space, my mental health and my family. Some fared better than others with the transition.

Chapter 44

Journal - June 4, 2013

110 days - My due date was a tough day. It was tough weekend. There is a rational part of me that knows how much Joe would have suffered. There's the rest of me that just misses him. It will never be better or fixed. The length of time since we lost our son will just keep growing.

I'm so glad I got that last video ultrasound. I had a lot of anxiety waiting for the appointment and worried that he wouldn't make it long enough for me to get those images and pictures. Normally you get those things at the twenty-week ultrasound but the technician had stopped recording after a few minutes and there were no pictures.

Sometimes those premonitions haunt me. It was like I knew. That first week after Joe died, I had waves of déjà vu. It was flashbacks of the birth and doctor visits but it felt like I had seen it all before and I wondered why I didn't see it all coming.

I didn't return the clothes I bought for Joe. I have all of Cole's clothes saved but I wanted Joe to have a few new things too. I thought if I had to return it, it would at least give me something to do so I wouldn't sit around crying all the time. Then one day, I had a burst of 'okay, let's deal with this grief today' shortly after Joe passed away and when I put my hand on the first hanger I felt the room start to tip. It's all packed away now.

Last week a conversation with a stranger likely saved our lives. We stopped to look at an apartment and a neighbour came over to our truck thinking it was her son's vehicle. We had a wonderful conversation. Something kept pushing me to ask her more questions. She was telling me all about her grandbabies and all the new ones on the way. I haven't been able to talk about anyone else's pregnancy but that evening, I kept asking for more details. Shortly after driving away we stopped at a red light in a big intersection and the watched the truck ahead of us barely miss getting hit as he scooted through to race the light change. A few seconds in the difference, it would have been us trying to catch that light. It seemed like a message. Or a gift.

That night we received another gift. A positive pregnancy test. I took five extra tests to confirm. We had to go to Planned Parenthood to get an official medical declaration to qualify for Medicaid to receive prenatal care from our current doctor. My state health insurance coverage stopped when I lost Joe and Dr. Porter wouldn't run the confirmation test if we couldn't pay for it.

At Planned Parenthood they sat with me to deliver the results and discuss my options. There was a form to fill out asking if I wanted to continue the pregnancy. Josh and I joked in the waiting room about the idea of planning a pregnancy and coming to Planned Parenthood to wade through the protesters in the main entrance. No, really folks, we aren't going in to have an abortion. Put your torches away. We actually just can't get medical care for Mom or baby unless we rely on this 'devil clinic' and the valuable medical services they provide to anyone who needs them.

We took my first pregnant belly photo on Joe's due date and posted it on Facebook. I know it's too early to announce it and so many things can go wrong but unless you've been where I am and know the mix of grief with anticipation, terror with joy, anxiety with hope, there is really no room to judge. Or maybe I've just learned that life is too short to listen to the judgments. I know I need the support of my friends and that is okay.

My due date is three weeks before the date Joe left us. I am carrying his Irish twin – which is actually supposed to be a derogatory term, but I see it as a blessing. There's something about shamrocks and all things Irish that keeps me connected to Joe. This blessing gives me so much comfort. We will meet again my sweet Joe.

An Irish Blessing

May the road rise up to meet you

May the wind be always at your back

May the sun shine warm upon your face

The rains fall soft upon your fields

And until we meet again

May God hold you in the palm of his hand.

Chapter 45

Journal - June 29, 2013

Four months, two weeks and one day - The question is upon us whether to run the MaterniT21 test for this pregnancy. I'll be ten weeks in just a few days and that's the earliest the blood work can be done. Joe's chances of having Trisomy 13 were 1 in 10,000. Depends on where you look for the information but basically we have a slightly higher or exactly the same risk of this baby having the same chromosomal abnormality.

I didn't test for anything during my pregnancy with Cole. The things they look for and the invasiveness to find out things we can't fix or control just wasn't worth the risk. The only reason we tested with Joe was to determine exactly the cause of his list of super powers. All it did was give him a life expectancy and a label so the doctors could decide if he was worth operating on.

The reassurance the test could provide would be nice. I

don't expect the exact same thing to happen. That's what most fears are based on - not new things that may happen but old things happening again. Would I even care if this baby has Down Syndrome or Edwards Syndrome? Only to the extent of the co-existing possibilities that go along with Trisomy 21 or Trisomy 18 but like the multitude of conditions that people walking this earth have, those are things I can live with. I could even live with Trisomy 13. Worst case scenario, I would just want more time than I had with Joe. Even if it was to get beyond 26 and a half weeks pregnant. Just more time.

On one hand there is this person that I would like to be who can manage pregnancy and does all the admirable things – no tests, no anxiety, absolute faith in everything working out. There is another person that lost a baby just four and a half months ago and was already kind of a basket case and has had everything I knew turned upside down. I want to hear the heartbeat every day and see an ultrasound scan every week and find a way to keep control in an uncontrollable situation.

The urge to do everything different is strong. So is the urge to change nothing for fear of inviting a jinx. I know that makes me somewhat of a nightmare as a patient.

A few weeks ago I had an appointment for a due date and viability scan. It was for late in the afternoon and by ten in the morning, I was climbing the walls. I called my OB/GYN and asked if I could get an earlier appointment. It was a double stressor because the appointment was where I went to see Joe that last time not moving on the screen.

Michele didn't miss a beat. She said it was out of the question and because it wasn't an emergency she wasn't even going to ask the doctor. I wanted to go to a less equipped facility but the advice from the bookkeeper was that she thought the doctor would want me to 'start off right this time around.' As though a chromosomal abnormality was something you can blame on a parent. You can't. It occurs just after the sperm and egg meet and divide. It's that early and it's nobody's fault.

I called the OB/GYN's office from my cellphone in my other hand and when another secretary answered, I hung up on Michele. Cathleen went straight to Dr. Porter and had an appointment for me in a few minutes.

As we were walking out the door to go to the earlier appointment, the phone rang. It was Michele leaving me a not so nice message saying I could call her back unless I had hung up on her on purpose.

I have to admit, I couldn't feel my toes or fingers as I called back. I explained to her that I was very anxious and she could have at least humoured my request and until she lost a child she was in no position to judge. She was yammering over me about wanting an apology. I hung up on her again.

My husband called back and spoke to her as gently as he could manage. He explained that her inattentive dismissiveness was just adding to my anxiety and if she was going to be a problem we would have to go to another care provider. She told my husband she expected an apology from me and one would not be forthcoming from her.

Chapter 46

The medical profession as a whole delivers news of a Trisomy much the way they would tell you that you have a terminal illness. It does not come with resources or education on how to accommodate that child's needs. If you were told you had a gifted genius on the way, all the Ivy league schools would send you a scholarship but those kids are equally atypical. There are so many medical and technological advancements every day and a child with a different way of living, eating, learning, or communicating is so much better equipped to survive and thrive but the phrase incompatible with life is thrown around and to a new expecting parent it only takes a suggestion to sway their decisions. A promise of a perfect baby if they just try again. Dr. Porter told me the statistics suggest that babies born after a loss are actually extra healthy. Kind of like an athlete who says he gave 110%. There isn't more than 100%. There is healthy or not healthy. And a baby who is loved and wanted counts. Not the next one. This one.

I don't want big pharma to get all pissed off at me since they are doing so well on the stock market but I think telling a couple who had not even heard the baby's heartbeat that their child's diagnosis is incompatible with life is a disservice. It's not diagnostic if there's a game plan in place to wipe the kid off the map based on the results. And if you think using the term game plan is paranoid, you haven't been sitting in a room wearing a johnny coat when they swarm in.

I got in touch with Maternal Fetal Medicine last year to ask if I could come and get some footage in one of the ultrasound rooms because I was working on a documentary about Trisomy 13. They didn't ask any questions about my angle or approach, they just had our old genetic counselor call me back to quote their policy on having no cameras in the facility.

I'm not an expert on Trisomy 13 or grief or pregnancy but I know how I felt and how I was treated. I know the pediatric cardiologist who had me alone in a room kept his hand inappropriately resting on my pelvic bone for the entirety of the procedure and then told me my baby wasn't worth saving. Nobody would have believed my word over a specialist. How easy to call me hysterical since I was carrying a baby with a chromosomal abnormality. It was as if I was already labelled mentally unfit because I chose to continue the pregnancy.

Fact is there are kids who live for years with partial, full and mosaic Trisomies. I don't know how many or for how long or what their lives are like but it happens and nobody is taking those numbers down. Radio Shack tracks anyone who buys batteries. Surely someone else wants to know this information about babies who are never given a chance.

Chapter 47

My 10-week ultrasound on my rainbow pregnancy went beautifully. Mobile Imaging was a smaller operation than Maternal Fetal Medicine but the waiting room was friendly and had some toys Cole could play with. The air didn't feel like it had been forced into the room. Janet the ultrasound technician patted my arm after it was over and said she understood my anxiety and was so glad she could fit me in early to reassure me. On the way out there was mixup with insurance information as it was a new location for us. Janet shooed us out the door telling me that she would be seeing me quite often until this baby arrived safe and sound and to just go home and get some rest. She said insurance was the least of our concerns and she'd see us in a few weeks.

When I got home from Mobile Imaging I called the office manager at my OB/GYN's office. I felt buoyed by the vote of encouragement we had just received. Not only was the baby growing and thriving but we met a person who seemed to agree that a little anxiety was normal after what we had been through and if there was a way to alleviate that, we should do it.

When Cathleen Porter said she couldn't comment on her co-worker's behavior I asked to talk to my doctor. Surely the man who had actually held Joe after Nurse Olivia delivered him just a few months ago would see the gravity of the situation.

Dr. Porter mentioned that the due date and viability scan showed a healthy baby. I brought the conversation back to Michele and he reminded me I should be very happy about the good report from the ultrasound. Nobody seemed to want to take responsibility for the person in customer service who was giving out medical advice and refusing to even entertain a request from a customer.

We weren't actually what you'd call paying customers though. On Cole we had private insurance and paid hundreds out of pocket for my care during pregnancy. On Joe I had state healthcare. Dr. Porter won't see patients who use Mainecare or Medicaid. If you're like me and were already a patient you get a soft pass. He still gets paid for his services but you don't get the deluxe package. You get Michele's opinions and don't expect an apology when she acts like a pig.

Chapter 48

Grant me the serenity to accept the things I cannot change,

the courage to change the things I can,

And the wisdom to know the difference.

You'll notice this does not request serenity from any particular denominational being or spirit or entity. Just to whomever or whatever may grant such things, please send me some wisdom. I can work with that. I'm still not really speaking to the almighty I grew up trusting.

As for prenatal care, leaving my current practice is terrifying. It truly feels like my OB/GYN was instrumental in me not dying during pregnancy. As though he is the only person with the knowledge to get a baby safely from within my womb to the outside world. His save percentage is hovering around .500 - I have one healthy baby and one that died. Nobody's fault but also to nobody's credit either - unless I can count all the nurses along the way and I may have done some of the work too.

Something else I have to consider is how empowered I am at that practice. After delivering my second child, I *should* feel as though I could deliver at home on the kitchen floor with a suction bulb and a pair of safety scissors. Maybe there's not a practice out there who would take me on with all my hang-ups and questions and demands. It's worth trying to find a place that will listen and coddle me. I am, after all, growing a tiny human.

Chapter 49

Journal - July 18, 2013

I've been mad at a lot of people and blaming them for the loneliness I feel in my bones but it's Joe that I miss. Yes I want the phone to ring but I want the hospital to call and tell me there's been a terrible mixup and I can come pick up my Joe anytime I want to.

Trisomy 13 sucks. It's not like one small thing or a repairable single defect, it's a system-wide, body-wide screw up that just demands a child face every obstacle possible. It gives Moms and Dads a run for their money - battling doctors and hospitals and genetic counselors and so-called specialists to prove your child is worth saving all before they even take a breath. He felt healthy in there to me.

Joe has been gone for five months and three days. Probably if I wasn't pregnant the details of my previous journey would not be so vivid but he is all I can think about.

It took a few minutes to find a heartbeat last week and I felt my stomach drop (probably why it was so hard to find the baby in there). In my head I was scheduling the D and C. I don't even know what that is but I was sure that's what I would need. I wondered if we would try again and how long we could wait and how much more time I had with my 36th birthday peeking around the corner at me.

I have no reason to believe there is anything wrong. I had no cord issues, placenta issues, cervix issues, preterm labor issues, not even gestational diabetes to contend with before. Really the only bad thing that has happened to me was that one time my baby died. It's ridiculous to be this worried.

Joe's Irish twin is chugging right along and growing despite my outward appearance of crazy. I'm due in late January and this baby does not have Trisomy 13, 18 or 21.

I struggled with having the MaterniT21 test done until I was certain in my own heart that the results would not make a difference. The idea of going through it all again terrified me but I didn't decide to try for another baby assuming he or she would be perfect. Waiting was awful and the flashbacks of waiting for Joe's results got overwhelming. I was not a tester before all this happened but after losing a child, I'm not the same person. It could have easily gone the other way.

My anxiety has decreased by about two percent since we

got the results. Some things about me obviously have not changed. At least I had a picture to get me through the wait.

I have to believe that Joe is watching over his family. That we will wrestle toys from my children when they fight and we will see them help each other onto the school bus.

I'm reminded of the Monkees song:

> *I thought love was only true in fairy tales*
>
> *Meant for someone else but not for me*
>
> *Love was out to get me*
>
> *That's the way it seemed*
>
> *Disappointment haunted all my dreams.*
>
> *And then I saw his or her face…*

Loss moms don't usually say "I'm having a baby" instead they say "I'm pregnant" because really that's all we know for sure. I read that somewhere the day I found out we were expecting again.

So I will repeat the mantra I kept while I was expecting Joe.

<u>Today I am pregnant.</u>

And maybe someday I'll be a believer again.

Chapter 50

Journal - August 9, 2013

I did something a little out of character last week. I went to see a psychic medium. Not that I don't know where Joe is – I guess I wanted to know if he was in turmoil or unhappy that I'm having a baby. And the verdict is…..dat dat dat dah….I have no idea. I know a lot of people try the same thing to find peace after a loved one dies and some people absolutely get peace from it. I did not. I kept waiting for something that only Joe would know or maybe to hear that someone else who had passed away was coming through. And alas, I am left with memories that I already had and what I think my loved ones would want to say.

I was on a Facebook page for lost babies and saw a medium who had a waiting list for 'readings across the miles.' Apparently she had suffered a loss as well so that gave her license to peddle to bereaved moms. It's a lucrative market. I went to someone who did not advertise, who was recommended by people who had great experiences there. I just didn't get a mind-blowing convincing read.

The weird thing was the conversation in between 'messages.' The stuff this woman talked about in passing resonated with me.

She talked about Joe's story impacting people. That people from all over were hearing about Joe and he was making a difference in a lot of people's lives. I had to ask if any of them would ever tell me or Joe's dad about that impact. She explained some folks are young souls and simply cannot see the world outside themselves. They see things like Joe's death only for how it affects them. They love chaos and will sometimes go out of their way to cause it. They are incapable of feeling empathy but not because they are bad people – they just have young souls who have not yet learned how to be, or act, or care in a way that's helpful to others.

This medium said maybe this new baby would be an easier channel for people to reach out and I had to ask – even though I wasn't really buying into the whole talking to the dead, messages from beyond idea – will Joe help me to forgive these people who have let us down when we needed them?

I know mediums aren't for everyone. I don't know that I

would ever go back or even if I would try again with a new medium.

The grief support coordinator keeps talking about doing the work – not avoiding the grief – and insists that a goodbye ritual is necessary for healing. She says even women who enter menopause are encouraged to do something to mark the end of their fertility because it, too, is a loss.

I've rolled my eyes each time she's mentioned those ideas.

I don't want to do a goodbye ritual because I don't want to say goodbye to Joe. When I 'sit with my grief' I just pray that I'll stop breathing so I don't have to feel what comes out. A month ago I finally got the guts together to get Joe's death certificate and it was a wreck. They had called him Baby Linegar and crossed that out and wrote Joe G. Morgan in there and then someone had written above the middle initial – "rayson." His name appears on one official document. I guess they thought getting it right was more than he deserved.

Chapter 51

Journal - August 15, 2013

It's been six months. I'm planning an online memorial. I've asked my friends at all corners of the earth to join me in lighting a candle at about the same time so that we can be joined in light and spirit. There's something about candle flames that make me feel a tiny bit better and we still couldn't fill a bathroom here locally.

Not that I'm comfortable with any of this all of a sudden. I'm turning inside out. It took about six different nights sitting in front of the computer searching for urns. I could go to another funeral home and see their displays but that's not on my list of capabilities either. I did finally find a small wooden memory box with the entire Irish blessing and it will have Joe's name engraved on it. His full name - Joe Grayson Morgan. I'm not ready to transfer the ashes. I haven't even opened the package they came in.

I ordered some candle holders and plaques with the Irish

blessing. Then I started having panic attacks again. The urge to get out of the house became overwhelming. I knew I should be here to accept the packages but I just wanted to go camping somewhere that I couldn't get even phone signal let alone mail.

Chapter 52

I got what I wished for. I didn't have to open the packages when they arrived. My upstairs neighbour went ahead and opened my mail. Her name was Victoria too. We met after she came pounding on our door the first night we moved in. She was yelling and threatening to call the cops. She put a call in to our landlord that inaugural night too and he asked us to keep it down with all the boxes and shuffling and walking on the floor.

When she opened the items I had ordered for Joe's memorial she ran to get the downstairs neighbour. Together they surmised what was in the box and realized that I might take Victoria's head off if I thought she had snooped on purpose.

The nice old lady I actually liked came to my door. She was a light worker and had tried a few times to give me breathing techniques and energy work. I was fine with the breathing but not ready to try to anything unsanctioned by the religious bodies. She did a masterful job of keeping me focused on the contents of the package and not the fact that something so personal had been violated by someone I couldn't stand.

The horror is not over for us but I have hope that someday it won't feel quite as bad or raw. Just as the panic attacks eventually pass, so will my fear that facing my grief will be the end of me. I have not dealt with Joe's death. I've gone through the motions and done all the textbook things a person should do to be healthy after a loss. But my experience is tucked way back in a place I'm afraid to go.

Josh keeps telling me this is not saying goodbye, it's finding a way to keep Joe in our lives. I've really only ever lost one person that devastated me nearly as much as losing Joe and I still remember watching his casket be lowered into the ground. I found some healing in giving his eulogy and helping plan his service. So I guess it's a matter of reframing this. It's not a memorial, it's a tribute. And it's a part of life just like birth is. I think a person's brain needs to see and touch death to really appreciate life. No question about it – this sucks. But it is nice at times to be in an empty room and feel someone I love beside me. That's comfort that even people who are alive and kicking can't provide.

Chapter 53

I had to give up on my Psychology degree. Dr. Eyeball eventually responded to the emails I sent when I was still pregnant with Joe. It was after he had handed down my final grade. Turns out I didn't do so well on the exam I cried all over. It brought my grade down to just below the requirement for it to count. I asked him for an opportunity to rewrite it. He told me I should not have written the exams and then he could have done something for me. That a rewrite was out of the question because it was against his policy and if he did it for me, it would start a trend of letting any student rewrite for any old reason and he wasn't willing to do that.

I wrote to his boss. I wrote to the president of the university. After checking with my other professors to ensure I was a good student deserving of fair treatment, my professor's boss offered to let me take the class again. The president of the university at least said she was sorry for my loss and feigned distress over this treatment of a bereaved mother/paying student. She assured me she would investigate and not rest until a remedy was in place that would ease this undue burden in my life. She left the job a short time later without ever sending me another word.

Chapter 54

Journal - September 15, 2013

Tonight we re-lit three of Joe's candles. One for the new baby, one for Joe and one for Cole – the three leaves in my lucky clover. We're watching a DVD of the ultrasound we had earlier today. Cole keeps saying 'Baby Joe!' and we have to keep reminding him, no, not Joe, new baby.

Joe has been gone now for seven months. We didn't throw away or hide the big brother shirts and we talk about how much we love him often. We are already a family of four.

Sometimes it feels like he's really gone and other days, it's like he's sitting beside me holding my hand when life gets too real. I've been extra anxious now that the baby is approaching the same size Joe was and the kicks are just as strong.

I wonder if this will be the last kick; if little one is getting enough of the things a baby needs; if we missed another Trisomy the tests can't pick up. Mostly I feel guilty for wanting a healthy baby, for not wanting another still, motionless child in my arms. I don't think I could survive it again.

Over the past couple of months I've been seeing a group of midwives who promised to focus on both mom and baby while I'm pregnant. I was upfront in the beginning about my anxiety, PTSD and fears. They reassured me time and again, we are here for whatever you need. Come in as often as you want to hear the heartbeat if that will help ease your mind. Chase us down the road if you see us in public if that's what you need. Call anytime. It only takes two minutes to drop some gel on your belly and put the Doppler on there. That's what we're here for.

I've also been meeting more and more loss moms whose stories haunt my nights and my days. I know the things that can go wrong. I know there are hundreds of other possibilities. I'm also in my first year of loss. I am a nightmare patient. I'm also a nightmare wife and friend. Some people have signed on anyway and are loving me through this process.

Two days ago the eldest dirt mother at the midwifery group read off all the dates that I've called in for that support they offered and told me that what I expected of the practice was abusive and they couldn't have one pregnant woman ruling the roost.

She had taken offense when I asked if I could start having ultrasounds every month. I'm approaching the time I lost Joe. There's only so much yoga a person can do to ease anxiety and sonograms are relatively harmless unless you are the rat in that study where they held the ultrasound in place for 72 hours.

Maybe I changed my mind about how many I wanted. I went from the none suggested by some folks to the same amount some of my mom friends had for much less reason than a previous loss.

My 'care provider' told me she would refer me this one time but unless it was recommended by the high risk doctors at MFM, that was it – she was not going to be directed by me. Then she asked in her best condescension 'do you understand what I'm saying?'

It flashed through my mind to spew ugly things at her about death and loss and grief and cold bitches who let a tiny bit of power convince them they have some magical ability to keep babies alive – but instead I stayed calm. I felt something in the room that kept my hand steady and my voice from cracking.

I had already spoken to the folks at Maternal Fetal Medicine who were not surprised to hear from me at 21 weeks and were bending over backwards to fit me in to check on my baby. And what do you know – given my history, they were more than happy to schedule me for each month from here on out for as long as I'm lucky enough to still be pregnant.

The midwives are the only act in town unless I want to do a home birth or go back to an OB/GYN. I can't imagine they aren't aware of that. I wanted a more empowered birth experience and I fail to see how cutting someone down is supposed to be helpful. Perhaps if they had returned my husband's calls when he tried to act as my birth partner and called for me. Or if the two ladies in the office the day I asked for a heartbeat check could have stuck around for a couple of minutes before taking their hour and a half lunch break, I would have felt supported.

I know at least a couple of people who read my blog regularly who will roll their eyes and pat themselves on the back for always knowing what a screw up I am. What a disappointment and wreck I've made of Cole's and my husband's life. Whether that exists in my head in the wee hours of the morning or if it's real, I don't know. What I do know is that being dismissed and accused of being abusive when I'm just asking for help puts me right back into those relationships where I'm nothing – someone whose birth was a mistake, whose existence is simply a scourge on humanity.

I already feel low enough. I have a son who looks to me for cues on how people should treat us. How to pick yourself back up when you fall down and when people are mean to you. I refuse to be anyone's doormat at least while he's watching. I owe it to him and Joe to take care of myself even when I am struggling to face the day.

Chapter 55

I left the midwives practice. I got a copy of my chart and brought it to the new clinic myself. That's how I found myself sitting in Maternal Fetal Medicine again.

Two older, robust women were in the waiting room including everyone in their conversation, poking at kids and discussing how often one of them was going to use the bathroom (I wish I was kidding). I didn't care even though we were all sat there for 45 minutes until one of them blurts out "How did I not know that, I'm so retarded."

A mom across the waiting room caught my disgusted look and she smiled that knowing look and pointed down at her tiny daughter in her arms and mouthed the words "I know, she has Down Syndrome."

I just sat there and cried.

So often over the course of my life, I have walked away from experiences feeling like a complete failure wishing I had said something but not wanting to rock the boat or be disliked. It hasn't gotten me anywhere. I still feel awful after I speak up but it does more damage to me when I stay quiet.

I didn't cause a scene in the waiting room because all I could think of was to point out the little girl who had Trisomy 21 and demand those ignorant women apologize. I'm not sure I handled it well to be honest. I feel like I let Joe down. I did go over and tell the mom about my little boy and congratulate her on the beautiful little miracle in her arms. That was all I was capable of at the time.

I'm a mom of a child with special needs. I didn't dodge that bullet because Joe died. You just can't see him with me. It hurts to the core when I hear the word retarded or even the more subtle things like pretending to finger spell or making noise as though you can't talk or make jokes about riding the short bus. It all amounts to the same thing and it hurts.

You know me though. Much braver in writing than in person.

Chapter 56

Journal - October 17, 2013

I don't have a clue who is going to deliver this baby.

I went to a fire station tour in our neighbourhood and asked what the protocol is if I'm home with a toddler when I go in to labour. Turns out they have a car seat on board and they are almost as equipped as a neonatal intensive care unit.

I had another checkup this week at the high-risk clinic. A few minutes after I arrived a pregnant woman and her mother walked in pushing a stroller with a kid about Cole's age. The pregnant woman refused to sit down and instead chose to lean against the wall staring into space. Same spot I picked when I lost Joe. She looked about 20-25 weeks along. She wouldn't look at her toddler who was chattering away to everyone in sight. They were all escorted inside by an ultrasound technician and about ten minutes later, the technician came out looking for the next patient. The previous family had been shuffled out the back. I have a hunch I know what their weekend turned into.

I thought about those encounters while I sat through my appointment at MFM. I was told about hospital policies and the chances of the doctor I've signed on with delivering my baby – one in 7. She covers two nights and one weekend out of the month. Except when she's on vacation. There are 6 other doctors who do rotations.

The high risk clinic is a part of Maine Medical Center which is a teaching hospital so the nurse was explaining what that will mean for me - residents and students and an audience of people with no direct impact on my health care. I brushed her off and said, no need to discuss that, I won't have residents involved in my delivery. Well that's not how it works, nurse continued, it's part of the hospital's setup, the residents have to learn somehow.

I replied, "Not to worry. I'll put it in my birth plan that I don't want residents."

"You probably shouldn't deliver at Maine Med then."

Forced from my docile, pregnant cocoon, I explained that my decision on where to deliver was made already and having delivered two babies there I knew a thing or two about what I could and should do, thank you, let's move on.

I'm almost glad she tried to give me advice because it left me feeling compelled to share what I know and have learned in the past few years.

1. You do NOT have to be touched or seen by a resident in a teaching hospital. You are not only allowed, you are entitled to see a real doctor.

2. You do NOT have to give birth in front of a team of students so they can see how it's done. Someone else can be on display if they choose – you don't have to submit to any public viewings by people not involved in your care.

3. Nurses don't know everything.

4. Doctors don't know everything.

5. Nobody knows everything.

6. Hospital policies don't supersede your right to privacy or qualified doctors.

7. If you request an actual doctor, the nurses may be irritated with you and it may take longer to see someone but you will get an actual doctor.

Chapter 57

Journal - December 15, 2013

Joe has been gone ten months today. Taking out all the Christmas lights is like unpacking memories of the time we had with him last year. When we put the tree up I thought my biggest concern was the unshakeable nausea. By the time we took the tree down, we knew Joe had Trisomy 13 and were being told we would never take him out of the NICU if he even survived to term.

It should be getting better with time but it feels more raw now more than ever. I can remember every detail as though it's still happening.

It helps that my oldest is so excited about every little detail of Christmas. He keeps catching me crying and asks "Are you sad again Mom?" It's almost as if each time I drift off, Joe sends me a little nugget to keep me moving forward. Old Christmas songs that on a regular day would do me in, I now have a very musically inclined toddler singing along with his own lyrics. I remember over the summer a few times that the rain would hold off until we were out of the park and I'd stop and thank Joe.

Now that I'm so very pregnant with Joe's Irish twin, the anxiety is overwhelming. It's a good thing I don't have a doctor who would take me seriously at this point. It's not the discomfort of having a five pound child trying to push an elbow through my belly button, it's the knowledge that right this second, the baby is okay and healthy. I would gladly submit to an induction or C-section. Partly because there were only six weeks of the past 15 months that I wasn't pregnant – and partly because I've heard so many stories about babies who were fine one minute and gone the next. Patience is hard to come by.

I finally found medical care for the remainder of my pregnancy. The clinic at MFM refused to take me on because of my demands and I ended up at the hospital clinic which is ironically made up almost entirely of residents and interns. There are also a lot of wonderful nurse practitioners and attending physicians. I have not met a resident yet. Turns out – I do have a say in my care. I was ready to throw in the towel and pass my body over for science but I do, in fact, have the right to refuse practice exams. Even at a teaching hospital. Even at a teaching clinic.

I've changed my name over to my partner's last name and changed the blog address too. Ten months ago the hospital wouldn't release Joe's body because the name on his death certificate didn't match my last name. It's taken a while but my name is the same as all my babies now.

My very best thoughts go out to all the loss moms whose stories have touched my life. The thought that I should be shopping for two kids this Christmas lingers on my mind every time I see a sparkling light or a blade of snow. This is a special kind of hell we are in and unless a person has walked in our shoes, they don't get it. So be kind to yourself, take the space and time that you need and pat yourself on the back for every minute you have survived without your baby. All this talk of family and togetherness and gratitude and love this time of year – I can't say I'm able to reach those heights. But please know you are not alone in your grief or sadness or loneliness. This sucks. I have so much to be thankful for but not having Joe here with us – in a word – sucks.

One holiday at a time, one month at a time, one breath at a time – is all that is required of any of us.

Chapter 58

I had been having Braxton Hicks contractions and feeling bloated and uncomfortable for about four weeks before Connor decided he was ready to kick his way out. The night before I was having hard pain about every 20 minutes. Cole was walking up and down the hallway wearing my slippers reminding me to breathe and rubbing my back.

I had an appointment at the clinic later that day but about an hour before we were supposed to leave I suggested we go in early and see if there had been any progress. Josh headed to the car with Cole and I said I'd be out in a second because I had to use the bathroom. Before they reached the front door I was buckled over the bathtub in pain and yelling for Josh. I felt like my intestines were exploding. It passed and I stood up to leave and buckled over the top railing of the stairs. I made it to the truck and another pain hit. I had two more on the 8 minute drive to the hospital.

Josh dropped me in front of Maine Medical Center while he went to park and another pain hit so I grabbed a tree branch to steady myself. I was next to the entrance and a lady walked past and asked if I was okay. I told her I might be having a baby and she said "Oh...well good luck" and walked away.

I told the receptionist she might want to put me in a room so I didn't scare all the first-timers in the waiting room. I still thought I had to use the bathroom.

A nurse practitioner came in and without putting a hand on me said honey you're in labour. I said "Nah."

She asked me to get on the bed just in case and I agreed but would only get on all fours. For some reason I pulled off my winter boots and pants and let her put a sheet over me. In seconds I was being wheeled down the hallway into the elevator and rushed up to labour and delivery. The nurse on the desk told the team that was surrounding my stretcher that they should have called ahead for a bed. I screamed "There's a fucking person coming out of me, get me a room!"

I was offered a better bed but when I got off the first one, I bent down in a yoga pose I had been practicing to ease the pain. It didn't work but I couldn't stand back up. Another nurse tried to push the prenatal monitor belt into my stomach to get a read on the baby and I pushed her away.

I had never been in so much pain in my life and there wasn't a break between contractions like they promised.

I let a nicer nurse put the monitor belts around my abdomen but I was still basically huddled on the floor. I asked for some ice chips and the seven people in my room just stared at me. An intern said she was there to check my dilation and I said sorry no interns. She started explained hospital policy and I warned her that if she checked me and said I was less than 6 centimeters, she wouldn't be allowed back in my room. She told me I was seven and a half.

It was while I was buckled on the floor in a deep pelvic squat that I thought I was going to die. I couldn't imagine where I was going to find the strength to deliver this baby and everyone in the room was just milling around looking at each other. Josh was keeping Cole busy across the room. I felt a warm sensation on my back and it was then that I felt Joe with me. Somewhere in my mind or heart I heard "Mom it's okay to do whatever you need to get this baby out here safely."

I asked for my attending nurse to come closer and asked what my options were for pain management. I got them all. An hour later I was propped up in the bed singing Ring of Fire. I wasn't feeling much of anything in that wonderful world of epidural numbness except for the emotions that the drugs can't touch.

The nurse noticed my contractions were off the charts and wondered why my water hadn't broken. No sooner had she said it when the room turned into a pool and folks were running in with mops and towels. The shape of the baby was so prominent in my deflated stomach but he still hadn't turned head down and he wasn't facing the right way.

The delivery team came in and told me it was time to push and got into position at the end of my feet and I said "You guys are all going to be so embarrassed when you see nothing is happening down there."

They told me to bear down anyway and all of a sudden my legs were up in the air. A stranger who refused to take care of me when I was pregnant because I had state healthcare was holding one leg and my husband was holding the other. Cole was playing on his stroller a few feet away and I heard someone say "I see the head. You need to PUSH Victoria."

I couldn't breathe. I was looking at the monitor watching the cardiac rhythms coming from my baby and I froze. Tears started pouring down my face and the attending doctor said everybody hold up. Something's wrong. Victoria what's wrong. Talk to me.

I said I can't do it. I just can't keep going. This baby is alive right now inside me and I'm afraid if I push him out, his heart will stop beating.

I have never felt that vulnerable or honest or scared or frozen in place as I did right then. I had my husband a few feet from me and an actual team of doctors and a healthy beautiful son just across the room. I remember Cole's face standing beside the hospital curtain that had been pulled across in front of the window when it got dark outside. He was looking at me unsure of what was going on and the whole room looked like an oil painting to me. The sounds were so far away and the beating on the monitor pounded and echoed in my brain. The bassinet that was waiting for my baby was so far beyond my reach and I had absolutely zero control over what was about to happen.

It was worse than the moment Dr. Porter couldn't find Joe's heartbeat. It was worse than walking over to Joe's bassinet. I think my own heart stopped beating.

Chapter 59

Journal - March 27, 2015

I don't see Joe anywhere or dream about him. He doesn't leave me any messages or signs. He's still gone. He isn't coming back. He should be here. He should be playing with his brothers. We should be arguing with doctors who don't believe babies with Trisomy 13 matter. But we are not.

As parents of a stillborn baby, we are never asked for pictures. We don't tell the birth story. The only safe place to grieve is around other parents who understand.

We were launched into another category when we had Connor. We became people who should no longer be grieving, who shouldn't complain about how hard it is with two, who are never quite happy enough or sad enough to anyone's liking. Pregnancy after loss sucks. It's harder than other pregnancies. Having had all three, I can say that.

We have lost friends. We are not the same people we were two years, two months and 12 days ago. With the solitary exception of losing Joe, we are better people now. Mostly because we don't give much of a fuck about anything anymore. What matters is within these four walls and people we care about get that. Anyone with good intentions is just fine with your personal space and boundaries.

The first time I took a R.A.D. class I was told that when someone stands too close to you in the grocery line and isn't paying for your purchase, they shouldn't have any issue with you asking them to step back. Should they cause a scene and call you a psycho or other derogatory name, they probably were trying to get your PIN or hear you tell the cashier your phone number for the Rachael Ray dishes. In other words they had bad intentions.

I happened upon such a woman at Burger King about a month ago. The place was empty except for her and my family of four. She had her order and was sitting down as I approached the drink machine with Cole. She decided she wanted more ice and proceeded to stand so close to me that when I exhaled her hair moved. Normally I would shrivel up. But since I was letting Cole pick his own drink and press the button, I took exception when she asked if she could get in there for just a second.

Keeping in mind, I was highly triggered that day for separate reasons. I was already worried about how many people had coughed on the drink lids, who didn't wash their hands back in the kitchen and how to eat chicken nuggets without actually touching them.

So I told her actually now's not a good time. We are getting our drinks.

Her hair didn't move. In fact she started breathing on my neck. So I took a deep breath and calmly said Ma'am, with all due respect, you are not making me go any faster. Could you please step back.

She stepped away...to get her tray and go to the counter and demand her money back because my family had 'ruined her dinner.'

With my 1- and 4-year-old looking on, I tried to play it cool.

Until I saw her storming back towards our table.

I stood up and got in her path and she inhaled deeply and put her finger up in my face to deliver the speaking to of a lifetime. But I was rude. I interrupted her. I told her that whatever she had to say was unimportant and that since I was there with my kids, she should back off. She leaned in closer. And started yelling. So I mentioned that should she proceed further, I would absolutely be pouring my drink over her head.

She kept yelling some nonsense about praying for me and where I was headed. My partner noticed things were not calming down and came over and stood between us and walked against her until she backed up.

He looked like the stew pot that Bugs Bunny was trying to stay out of. All I could see was her trying to get around him to get at me.

She finally grabbed her now takeout bag of Burger King cuisine and I guess she could see me hyperventilating. She leaned in and said "You brought this on yourself."

I'll admit it crossed my mind to go scream at her I HAVE PTS-FUCKING-D, MY BABY DIED YOU ASSHOLE.

And in my Canadian-born paranoid pacifist brain, I wondered if she had a gun in her Toyota 4Runner.

She did not have good intentions. In fact, when I saw her ahead of us complaining and asking for a refund for the 17 cent salad dressing, I should have gotten a clue that she was out for a fight. Why she chose the 5-foot-woman with the two small children and an already panicked face, I have no idea. Maybe I am an easy target.

To look at us from a distance, we have two boys. Connor has no idea there was a baby before him. Cole knows that sometimes a baby comes out of Mama and sometimes they die before they come out. I want to tell the story of the baby who is missing from that picture.

I'd love to make a documentary about Joe and Trisomy 13. I don't expect it will help anyone understand how it feels to lose a baby. I doubt it will convey the range of emotions it brings out to have a baby after a loss. What I hope to accomplish is to help some parents tell the story of the children they lost. To have some record that even though you can't see them at the playground with their brothers and sisters, they were here, they mattered and they had names.

It would include images of us with our families and there will be interviews and poems and letters. There will not be pictures of lost babies, there will be video tributes that we can watch again and again. And maybe it will take some of the sting out of the birthdays and the death anniversaries.

Over the next few months I am learning to use the equipment to make my documentary a reality. The local television station has been lending me gear and teaching me to use it. I have a Vimeo page and a YouTube channel and projects in the works to get better at filming, interviewing and editing.

Perhaps I'm wasting everyone's time. Big deal. I'm following the tiny little voice in my head that keeps telling me I'm creative and my ideas are worth looking into. It reminds me that the folks who take time out of their day to help a complete stranger are the ones who count.

Maybe the assholes of the world are nice to someone else. The saying that someone can't make you feel inferior without your consent is bullshit. Sorry Eleanor Roosevelt. Maybe it is my own personal issue if I feel bad about someone's actions. But I don't need to stay there. That's the part that's missing. You can get out of there.

I don't see signs from Joe. I have physical, psychological and emotional scars that will never go away. Turning that into an excuse to follow my heart is my choice. If you want to call that a sign, that's up to you. For me, I make a point of thanking him every time I feel a rush of happiness or dodge a bullet. I have a guardian angel. This is my way of paying tribute to my lost baby and to my babies who survived.

Chapter 60

We found a place to live out in the country. Our upstairs neighbours kept calling the cops on us when the kids would run across the floor. They made noise too. Mostly on Friday nights when they'd run out of booze or drugs and throw each other around the room and he'd storm down our back stairwell and scream "I hate you more than anyone I've ever met in my entire life. You're such a fucking bitch!" After that particular exchange we called the cops ourselves. The next morning as I carried groceries with Cole and the baby the female occupant leaned over our back stoop and told me I better not call the cops anymore. I told her she should go inside and not start anything in front of my toddler or she'd be sorry. I went to the car to grab my digital recorder. It would have come in handy when the cops showed up a few minutes later since they were there to cite me for uttering threats. They went and talked to her too but with no evidence, they told us both to stay out of trouble.

I went to the police station a few days later to get advice. I wore my R.A.D. shirt so they'd know I was one of the good guys. A lovely gentleman officer sat down with me on a bench and said he'd rent his property to us but it was already taken. Then he suggested that just like I teach women in self-defense class, sometimes the best response to violence and aggression is avoidance. Just get my family out of there. He said he knew that wasn't fair but reminded me to ask myself what it was that I wanted to see happen.

The new place was on a quiet cul-de-sac with an enormous front and back yard and a full basement to play in when it was cold outside. The pellet stove had a window with a silver coil on the end of a wrought iron handle. It was $1200 a month (American) and we had to get a cosigner to get in. It galled us to ask but we were very much about looking at the bigger picture at that point and what was best for the kids. So we called my mother-in-law and boy was she eager to help us out. She even offered to come help us on moving day. She couldn't lift any boxes or cook and she wasn't allowed to change diapers but whatever else needed to be done, she'd be there.

After picking her up at the airport we went to Walmart. She held Cole's hand on the way in and I was walking ahead with Connor in my arms. I heard Cole tell his grandmother that we had all been excited about her visit and had been having chats about her. She said oh yeah, what have you been saying. He said Oh, like about who's going to be changing my diapers... (dramatic pause, chubby toddler hand extending his pointer finger of the hand she wasn't holding directly at her).....not you.

I wanted to crawl under the pallet of paper towels in the aisle but I kept on walking. It wasn't until the end of her helpful visit that she voiced her concerns about my diaper rules. She advised me that I was messing up my children's sex lives because they would most likely find themselves in a situation with a girl perhaps in their twenties and they'd stop and say "Sorry, nobody's allowed to touch me there."

The middle part of the visit though found us alone together in a U-Haul pickup. I was driving and my lost baby came up in conversation. She said she had something to ask of me and she understood completely if it was out of line. She said when Joe died, Josh and I had each other and even though she was married and had her parents back in North Carolina, she felt there was nobody who really understood what she was going through when her grandson passed away and this loss happened to her too and she never got to see him or have anything of his to hold onto and she was wondering if I might give her some of his cremains.

I don't know how I would have reacted had I not been in the middle of an intersection turning onto the Million Dollar bridge but that's where we were and I took a deep breath. The thought of breaking the zip tie and opening up that little plastic bag that held what was left of my son to separate some of it and send it off with a woman who viscerally hated me and who I had never felt I could trust made me want to drive into the bridge abutment. Just step on the gas and impale her with a concrete telephone pole.

I gave her a speech that I can't even remember. I know there was something about how that wouldn't make her feel better, that this was the nature of grief, the unrecognized potential of a lost child, that even with something of Joe's to hang on to, I still knew they were just items and that he was never coming back and that essentially that was the hardest part of all.

The most difficult part of that conversation was not that it invalidated my experience as a grieving mother, or as her son's wife or even that I was trying so hard to piece my life back together for her other grandsons but it was that it happened when no one was around. That I could never truly convey the horror of this woman sitting beside me in a rental truck - who just days earlier had paid for said vehicle while flirting with the cashier and told my son to call her Mary Ann so the cute guy wouldn't know she was a grandmother - was the same woman who dared to tell me this happened to her too. All I had left of my child was in a 4X4X2 inch box and she wanted me to desecrate his resting place so that she might feel better about <u>her</u> loss.

If I can convey anything in this book to the family of a woman who has lost a child it's these three indisputable truths. One. It is not up to anyone else to decide that losing a baby may have been for the best. One day I might reach that conclusion but you never ever get to say that. Two. This did not happen to anyone else but the mother and father and siblings (in that order). Your grief, no matter how bad you think it is, is nothing compared to theirs. It's less than nothing. It's not even worth mentioning. And Three. Unless someone hands you an urn of cremains for that lost child, assume you can't have any.

Chapter 61

Journal - June 19, 2015

When my husband was diagnosed with cancer two weeks ago, it felt like a freight train had run over our feet. As if we had escaped death but that our lives were mangled beyond repair...again. That's how it feels to hear someone you are raising children with has a 'good' kind of cancer. Not benign or unaggressive or slow-growing. It was malignant, aggressive and fast-growing. But apparently it was known to respond well to treatment.

It was exactly how I imagined a diagnosis like that would go. At times it seems fake. At other times I wondered if the results were wrong and he really had days to live. I found myself wondering if this was the last time he'd wrestle with the boys. Or if he'd get to finish grad school and be a teacher like he had always wanted. And I wondered if it was okay to think about myself at all.

I have been finding this experience to have a lot of

similarities to Joe's diagnosis. The not knowing and the waiting and the behavior or lack thereof from the human beings around us. There were also positives.

We had relatives/friends in Tennessee that we met at a family reunion send care packages for the boys with a gift card for pizza.

A woman I used to teach R.A.D. with came with me and the boys to the hospital and missed a day of work to be there. It was the first time I had seen her since I was pregnant with Cole five years ago.

A woman I met at grief support when we lost Joe two years ago came by with lunch and toys for the kids while we waited to meet with the doctor for the pathology report.

Friends and family I haven't heard from in years emailed to make sure I had their phone numbers in case I needed to talk.

We got a card in the mail from Josh's 90-something year old aunt to wish him a speedy recovery. We were on prayer lists across the Bible Belt.

My aunt Caroline sent me 200 tea bags from Newfoundland so we could have a decent cup of tea 'together' whenever I needed it.

People made time for us. It didn't change what we were going through but it made it a hell of a lot easier to put a smile on for the kids and carry on as though things were mostly normal for them. The kids in turn made us laugh, kept us busy and reminded us why cancer can go fuck itself.

If someone you know is going through a cancer (or Trisomy) diagnosis, let me tell you how their day looks. They probably aren't getting much sleep. They still have to eat. There are doctor's appointments that are difficult to bring kids to. There are hours to fill that would be made easier by a visit to play with the kids. They are already thinking about what's happening so don't be afraid to get in touch for fear that you'll remind them of it. It's okay to say you are praying for them. It's even nicer to say I just sent your house a pizza.

Years ago we all used to live near our families and the phone and mailbox kept us in touch with people far away. Most of us are now the ones living far away. Our relationships and our physical and mental health are suffering. Don't underestimate what a small act of kindness can do for a family going through something awful.

Last week we went to Marden's, a discount store here in Maine that sells salvaged merchandise. We only carry debit cards with us so the giant gumball machine at the door was a huge disappointment to my oldest son because we didn't have change. When we got to the car I decided to grab the only quarter out of the parking meter money and go back inside with him. He watched the ball of sugar roll down the big spiral and he popped it straight into his mouth. He started chattering about what flavor it might be when it rolled out of his mouth and across the floor. It sucked. I know it was only a gumball but goddammit, give the kid a break already.

Then I heard a woman saying "ohhhhhhhh noooooooooooooo!" I thought she was angry that we hadn't yet picked it up off the floor but she came out from behind a pile of stock and said "Hey buddy, I saw what happened. Do you have another quarter?"

I don't know if I said any words before she reached in her pocket but all she had was two dimes, a nickel and two pennies. And she still gave it to him. She told him to go ask the customer service desk to trade him for a quarter. I braced for the sales associate to explain that they couldn't open the cash register unless we bought something.

Wrong again.

The next employee was wonderful too. She bent down to Cole's eye level and gave him the quarter and he said thank you and got a new gumball and skipped back out to the parking lot. His day was made. We're headed there today to give her a thank you card at Cole's request. I think that's a great idea because maybe she's having a rough day for some reason.

We meet with oncology tomorrow. Josh is officially a cancer patient. We are a cancer family. Years from now the kids will say 'oh yeah my Dad had that but I don't remember much about it.' This same type used to be a death sentence. We've come a long way. I wonder if the folks who are doing cancer research ever had a rough day that was made better by a quarter or a pizza or a phone call. Maybe the kids will remember those things. I know Josh and I sure will.

Chapter 62

Victim Services paid for my first therapist when I was in my late teens in Newfoundland. They set aside money for complainants in a court case and they keep it for a few years in case you change your mind and accept the help. Carol Ann Canning was a social work professor at Memorial University and she gave me tools to battle Obsessive Compulsive Disorder that I still use. She said if you starve compulsions eventually they die. She told me that washing your hands when they get dirty is perfectly acceptable. And because we had limited time, she didn't want to go down my list of triggers, she just wanted me to know how to deal with them when they came up. She told me that issues are like toys on a shelf. In rough times they all fall down and we learn in therapy to slowly put them back up. As we move through life, they will inevitably fall again but we become faster at putting them back where they belong.

I had a session with a speech language pathologist at the Miller Center in St. John's who I was referred to because of my trouble swallowing when I get anxious. Within a few minutes of meeting her I shared that I had been abused and had a fear of vomiting. She asked for details of the abuse and declared "Oh well that's where your fear of having things in your mouth comes from." And then she joked that it was a good thing she hadn't told me the stain on the chair I was sitting in was from a kid that had thrown up in her office. Ha....ha.....ha...

I had a counselor in St. John's named Sheila in my 20s who gave me physical tips on surviving an abusive relationship. When I joked and made light of it she told me about a patient who also laughed when she got uncomfortable and ended up with a pen sticking out of her temple when her partner stabbed her. She warned me to never fight on the side of the room away from the exit. She told me to be aware of the deadbolt and whether it was in the locked position should I need to open it quickly. I ended up using her advice many times before I got out of that relationship. She didn't care that I was writing articles in the newspaper about my big wedding. She heard what I said about my life and gave me tools to use to take care of myself.

I had a counselor in Maine who shared details of other patients' sessions. She told me I wasn't stable enough to write a blog or share my story. When my husband's boss would hit on me at parties she would tell me that I was inviting it in some attempt to sabotage my relationship with Josh. When I stopped seeing her she started relentlessly emailing me telling me she had never collected my copay and that I was preventing her from paying her bills.

In my 30s, I started seeing a counselor a few months after I had Cole. I hadn't been sleeping because I was checking on the baby all night long afraid that he had stopped breathing. I followed all the rules about putting him on his back to sleep and I never napped with him and there were no stuffed animals in his crib. I asked at my six week postpartum checkup about counseling and was referred to a clinic just down the road from the doctor's office. We agreed not to call it postpartum depression because I wasn't disconnected from the baby and I was showering on a regular basis so instead, my OB/GYN listed postpartum anxiety on my chart.

I called to make an appointment and the secretary told me there was a guy who seemed to have a lot of fun with his patients because she would often hear laughter coming from his office. She advised me he wasn't a specialist in postpartum anything but that he was a good therapist.

I saw Tim Frost once a month for the next year. Then my second pregnancy started off different. I didn't feel like I had on Cole. At about nine weeks I caught a bug and threw up thirteen times but it wasn't at all the traumatic event I thought it would be. I was worried about the baby though and I joked to three different people that getting so dehydrated would probably make the baby come out with six fingers on each hand. So I had asked for an ultrasound just to be sure everything was okay. The image on the screen didn't look like Cole had at that gestational mark. It looked all jumbled together to me.

I started going to counseling twice a month. I wanted to be in better shape than I had been for the first year and a half of Cole's life. I still didn't talk to most of my family and I was fighting with my in-laws regularly and I had severe doubts that I could ever finish a degree which was problematic since I had just gone back to school.

When the ultrasound confirmed some trouble with the pregnancy, I started going to see Tim once a week. After Joe died, I went twice a week.

For the first month after we lost Joe I had persistent anxiety attacks and constant nausea. I talked to Tim about possibly medicating. I wanted to know what my options were and since he couldn't prescribe anything he referred me to a nurse practitioner in his office. She was an asshole. (see chapter 43)

When I went back to my OB/GYN for my six week checkup he prescribed Ativan for me. He had a new nurse who told me how much she loved my new green New Balance sneakers. Then she said I also really like your bra. I was having an internal exam at the time.

When I was upright and dressed, I asked the doctor how much was a dangerous amount of Ativan to have in the house for an adult. I reassured him that even though I sometimes had bad thoughts, I was seeing a counselor and he had nothing to worry about. I asked him how much was dangerous for my toddler if he happened to find the bottle. My OB told me that it was far less for a toddler so we agreed that he would call in just ten pills at a time for me.

That was the first professional that I told about my troublesome thoughts. I made jokes about how much Ativan it would take to kill me. He still prescribed them and he never followed up on my comments.

I talked to my grief support group leader and she said she was aware that my OB was not great at catching postpartum depression cases. She said he was a highly recommended doctor but he missed the boat on mental health issues in new mothers.

Through various fallouts and reconciliations with family members and friends alike, Tim was there. I looked forward to our sessions and to discussing things that Josh just couldn't possibly understand. I saw nine general practitioners through staff changes and relocations and personality conflicts, two obstetric/gynecologists, four midwives and a team of 16 nurse practitioners and interns through three pregnancies in eight years. For five and a half years the only constant in my life was my therapist.

Chapter 63

Alan Hudson was the last doctor I saw in Maine. After I decided to remove myself from the Maine Medical System and moved my entire family's care to Mercy Hospital, Dr. Hudson was actually the second doctor I saw after the first guy got promoted. I was exhausted telling doctor after doctor how I was feeling and never really getting anywhere. He was an osteopathic physician and when I would go to his office with the right side of my body frozen from my neck to my hip, he'd invite me to sit on the examination table and a few clicks and pops later, I was completely mobile and pain free.

Sometimes I'd get it on the left side. He discovered trouble in my hips that was actually making one leg shorter than the other. A cough and a deep breath and a pop and that was fixed too. He said I was the only patient who found those procedures hilarious but I could not stop giggling. It was as if he was releasing years of pent up tension from my body.

When I told him I wasn't sleeping, that I would wake up choking on air and dry heaving an hour after I fell asleep each night and that during the day I was constantly nauseated, he investigated. He sent me for an ultrasound on my heart and a sleep study. He prescribed a host of medications for me to try that I could never get up the nerve to swallow but when I'd go back and tell him that, he didn't get mad. He'd suggest something different.

My therapist told me I was having panic attacks in my sleep which Dr. Hudson said was physically impossible. I repeatedly asked my therapist for physical techniques to calm myself when I had panic attacks but he never taught me any and he never sent me to anyone who could teach me. When I started exercising on my own, he said he hadn't suggested it because I wasn't the sort of person who exercised. (I was a trained fitness instructor in Canada and I was a self-defense instructor for the entire time I knew him.)

The doctor at the sleep clinic suggested that if it wasn't my heart or lungs causing me to wake up each night that maybe I had postpartum depression. Even though my kids were six and three, he had a friend who experienced it seven years after giving birth. I explained that I had been in therapy but that I had become more of a friend to my therapist. He relayed a story about a friend of his who had a massive heart attack because he only casually mentioned some pain he was having but that his friend, a cardiologist, hadn't thought much of it.

Two weeks later when the results came back from the sleep clinic, Dr. MyFriendHasThat very gently suggested that I was exhausted and needed some rest. He also mentioned that if I had a therapist already and was feeling the way I described that maybe it was time for a new one and I was clearly depressed.

Chapter 64

In January of 2017 I had sat in Tim's office and told him that I was having suicidal thoughts that were scaring me. I had told four other people the same thing, three of which had no idea how to react. But the fourth person asked if I had a safety plan with my therapist and if I had been honest with him about my feelings. I asked what a safety plan was.

She explained that I should have a list of emergency numbers to call if I felt overwhelmed or like I was going to hurt myself. That I should know which hospital to go to and what to tell them. And that at the very least my therapist should have given me a way to reach him or a crisis line. I had none of those things. Tim had never really taken me seriously. He kept saying I wasn't the type to kill myself. I had voiced concerns that if I ever asked for help that child services might declare me unfit to care for the kids. He reassured me that if that happened, he would call and straighten them out.

When I started my Masters later in 2017 I noticed the school offered free counseling and decided to give that a shot. I met with an intake counselor who asked me all the basic questions like was I afraid that my other kids might die. I answered honestly. No, they are perfectly healthy. And, she asked, how often do you worry about them being taken from you. Because ultimately, that's losing them too right?

I went home and told Josh about the session and he pointed out something I had not even considered before. The fear I was carrying around with me was that if I asked for help or disclosed those horrible, isolating feelings that someone might worry about the kids safety. Josh said, "You know you're not a single mother with mental health issues right? If you got into trouble, I'm here. They might come knock on the door but when they see there's another parent here, to care for you and the kids, they would walk away."

I called Tim's office and cancelled all my appointments.

Maybe I had been a difficult patient to read. Sometimes to avoid something uncomfortable, I would make a joke or I'd jump out of my seat to do an impression of a person who had crossed my path. But there were other times when a story about my sex life would be far too interesting. Sometimes he would make jokes about how easy it must be for Josh to be an out of work student with no responsibilities.

Once in a while he'd make a joke about intimate details that I had shared about my life and laugh so loud that I was sure his secretary could hear him. I wondered if she was telling new patients that he was in there doing a good job with me.

When Tim called to see when I was coming back I told him I was really confused and frustrated. I wasn't getting any better and I was tired of other professionals telling me to get a new therapist. Just in the past six months I had been staying up until 5 am each night and I started two unrelated companies and three Facebook groups and quit a Master's program, got accepted into a second program only to change my focus at the last minute and start a third program. I asked why he didn't consider that a manic episode.

He told me that he slept very well at night knowing he did a good job as my counselor. He said sometimes just before making a leap forward patients can regress and have a host of bad symptoms flare up.

I told him I needed time to think. He said I could make an appointment anytime and if too much time passed, he would call again. He hasn't.

Chapter 65

I met Mark White at school around Christmas 2016. He had PTSD too and also like me, he was getting tied up in knots with Disability Services and trying to finish his degree. I saw instructors and administrators pick at him like they did with me and once I even saw him have a panic attack that made him leave class and wander around campus which he later couldn't remember. I called Josh and said simply "I'm not the only one."

One day while Mark and I were talking he invited me to his car. He took a vaporizer pen out of a little velvet bag and asked if I was okay with that. I had never seen one before and he laughed at me. When his medication kicked in he explained that he and his wife had been anti-drug their whole lives but even she would sometimes say "Oh my goodness Mark, go have a toke." He told me about the new strains of marijuana that were cultivated to contain high levels of CBD and barely any TCH which is the one that gets you buzzed. He offered to share if I ever wanted to try it.

I relayed the entire conversation to Josh when I got home and we started researching what conditions justified a prescription for cannabis. One of the first on the list was Post-traumatic Stress Disorder (PTSD). It wasn't covered by insurance but you could pay $300 out of pocket to see a doctor. The card was good for a year and you could buy whatever you wanted to try. They had some education programs but it was really up to the individual.

I didn't have much hope when I crawled through the holidays that year and finally made an appointment at the beginning of January. I wasn't really functioning and Joe's birthday was right around the corner.. My therapist warned me that medical marijuana didn't work for everyone and might have an anxiety enhancing effect on me. I ignored him.

Integr8 clinic in Falmouth had Himalayan salt lamps and soft lighting and everyone was so nice. I felt empowered just being there. Not judged.

The nurse I spoke with said she saw miraculous changes in people and some even claimed that cannabis saved their lives. I wasn't optimistic and I was afraid to try anything but by then I was desperate for a day without nausea and panic attacks and I would have paid for a good night's sleep. Medical cannabis helped with so many of my symptoms and instead of doping me up I was able to think clearer and I could remember the times I used it unlike Ativan which made things foggy in the moment and blurry in the recollection. It helped with my appetite, it took the edge off my anxiety and it helped with my gut issues considerably.

It did not, however, erase the underlying stress that was causing my symptoms. It only took a couple of times where it didn't work for me to lose faith in it as a cure-all. I still had work to do.

Chapter 66

I called Dr. Hudson's office with the worst frozen shoulder I
had ever experienced and spent half an hour on the phone
with the on-call nurse. When I explained that my muscle
spasms showed up when I was stressed and just got
progressively worse, he suggested taking Ativan until I could
see the doctor. THAT was miraculous. He said the drug
used to be administered as a muscle relaxer in emergency
rooms.

When I saw Dr. Hudson I told him about the weed and the
Ativan and how both medications sat in my medicine cabinet
mocking me. It was like a war raging in me when I would
even think of using either one. I saw it as a failure to need
anything at all. I'd negotiate that if I could make it for 30
more minutes, maybe I'd feel better. I'd spend an entire day
luring myself away from something that could straighten me
out in minutes when I actually gave in and took it.

I was so much more gentle with myself when the medicine
kicked in. The judgement about needing help disappeared

and I could think about eating and I was a much better wife and mother. I was afraid of becoming dependent, I was afraid of running out and I was terrified that I would lose my current medical team and end up with a doctor who wouldn't refill my prescription.

Dr. Hudson, however, listened to every word I said and then he took a deep breath and asked if I had ever considered Mindfulness-Based Stress Reduction. I told him that sounded horrible and the idea of sitting still was worse than having my anxiety chase me around all day. He laughed and agreed with me but he said this is the way things are headed. So many of us are running here and there and none of us are willing to slow down and be with our thoughts or our traumas and that's where a lot of our conditions get their start.

My last doctor had made me sign a medicine contract of some kind promising that I would not sell my narcotics and I would not call his office asking for more before it was time and I would surrender my medication to them anytime they requested to see what I had left in the bottle. That doctor sent me home with a script for 0.5 mg Ativan every 8 hours as needed and he gave me ten pills......to last me a month.

When I told Dr. Hudson him how much Ativan I had taken in

my lifetime he laughed again and sent me home with a real prescription and no contract and suggested I look up the MBSR class. It was a short term and a long term plan.

Chapter 67

Reiki sessions were free for current patients at the cannabis clinic. It was desperation that got me in the door. With a full bottle of medicine and a vile of AC/DC cannabis oil in a vaporizer pen, I was still caught between wanting relief and fear that I would run out and need it even more than I already did.

I was starting my day afraid to put my feet on the floor. The panic attacks would kick in and I couldn't think straight. It had been three years since I lost Joe at that point and I was angry at myself for still hurting.

The nausea was the worst. I knew I wasn't sick. But I felt as if I could bend at the hip and lose my breakfast, lunch and last week's supper if I breathed the wrong way. I couldn't play with the kids, I couldn't function. The cannabis had eased the anxiety and the rolling tummy but I was frozen in place afraid to use it. The Ativan worked but only if I could convince myself to open the bottle.

When I walked into the clinic and asked about a Reiki session I was almost broken. I had cancelled the first attempt when I saw a man's name on the appointment confirmation. Funny how the mind plays tricks on you when you're sleep deprived and born anxious.

Reiki doesn't actually require contact. A practitioner can hold his or her hands a few inches above your body and it will have the same effect - which is relaxation.

I carry pain in my belly and tension in my neck. Long term anxiety hits me first in the gut. If I am about to go on stage or have to face someone I'm afraid of, you'll find me in the bathroom. If I get bad news, I get a rumbly in my tumbly in about 60 seconds.

If I don't deal with my feelings or get the anxiety under some control, it creeps to my neck, shoulder and hip and I can't drive or turn my head or get to sleep.

Reiki helped me with all those things.

It freaked me out at first and I wondered if we were summoning something awful until I realized how many religions use it, even if they would never call it Reiki. During all the sacraments, there is a laying on of hands. When the minister addresses the congregation, they hold up their hands palm out. When healers go visit the sick, there is most often something to do with the hands touching or being held over the person who is suffering. The cool touch of my mom putting her hand on my forehead when I had a fever....there is healing power in the hands of those with good intentions. I could be wrong but it changed my life. Or saved it. However you might choose to look at it. I didn't feel like I was ever going to get better - that I was permanently broken and the trauma of losing Joe had done irreparable damage. Which was problematic because I still had two little boys who needed me.

Chapter 68

I felt like a leper when I talked about Joe during class
introductions at Mindfulness-Based Stress Reduction. We
were supposed to tell why we had chosen to take the class
and I heard myself saying "I lost a baby four years ago and I
think it's time I faced that." The folks who said they were
taking the class because they had just gone gluten free kind
of looked at their feet. The lady who was teaching the class
came up to me afterwards and thanked me for sharing
because she had lost a child too.

I didn't want to go back. The meditation exercises made me
itchy and people beside me were the loudest breathers of all
time. I had Josh call and ask for a refund or a credit to do it
another time and the teacher refused. So to not waste the
$250 I went back. I was the met at door with a hug and a
warm "I'm so glad you came back" from the facilitator.

I wasn't able to complete all the homework and I skipped a
couple of classes but I signed up for another session and got
a few takeaways that I have found to be very effective. I

learned to do meditative breathing while I sweep or do dishes or knit or do yoga. I now have 45 different poses that allow me to listen to what my body and spirit are trying to tell me. Most often it says "Fuck This Shit" but sometimes I can just stop and feel my feet on the ground and be still and observe my thoughts like passing clouds. It's not about finding solutions but about taking a tiny, little break from the incessant intrusive and disruptive thoughts. Because no matter what's going on, it can wait until I take a breath or two.

MBSR was the hardest thing I've ever tried. Perhaps if I hadn't left my grief for so long it wouldn't have built up in the way that it did but I was really fucking sad about losing my son. I was angry at all the assholes who got to have healthy babies. I still felt an ache in my belly that was so wide I thought I could crawl inside it myself and disappear. Sometimes I wouldn't even realize how much it hurt until I would try to say just one sentence about my experience. I would go from someone who couldn't cry even when I wanted to into a person who had tears streaming down her face just over some words.

Intellectually I felt I had dealt with my loss. I told myself again and again that I had done the work. I got through another pregnancy and I was bathing on a regular basis and feeding my kids. What did the world expect of me beyond that?

Then last Fall I invited a woman who was organizing a walk for lost babies to be on my public access show. I had done 8 episodes by then but never anything about loss. It was the first time I pulled out of an interview since I started doing them in high school. I had been so proud of myself that I was producing a show and had never had to cancel on anyone. I never let my mental issues get in the way when it really mattered. Until I had to meet with a woman who had lost a baby to stillbirth.

It's difficult to take time to grieve when life keeps moving forward. Eventually, at least for me, I had to look back at what was chasing me because I couldn't run anymore.

Chapter 69

My old therapist told me once that I wasn't very good at finishing things.

I gave up on the Psychology degree at USM. I realized I didn't want to be a therapist bad enough to take that anatomy class with Dr. Eyeball. I switched majors three more times before I found my calling. It was the connection with people that I enjoyed whether it was doing interviews or teaching R.A.D. and abuse prevention or writing. I liked helping people and empowering them to speak their truth and defend their space and loved ones.

My advisor at the time liked to have closed door meetings with me. I knew that was unusual because the people he had in there before me always had the door wide open. He was also my instructor for some writing classes where I divulged a few personal details in my assignments. He was someone who made my skin crawl and stared a little too long when he thought nobody else was looking. There was one class where we all sat in a circle with small tables in front of our chairs and while the rest of the class was talking to each other's faces, I had a crotch in tight pants being pointed and squirmed at me while he made weird eye contact.

He was also, unfortunately, in charge of assessing whether previous work counted towards my degree and he said nothing I had ever done qualified. Radio and television and newspaper work, all nothing. Even courses I had taken he rejected. I asked for a different advisor. Old PervyTrousers was pretty angry but bullies usually are when you tell them to stop.

After reviewing my transcript and resume my new advisor Adam Bennett pointed out that I was just two classes from a degree in Communication and I graduated the following semester.

When I started producing Ounce of Prevention my old alma mater came asking if they could run a profile on me in their Alumni newsletter and the marketing they send to new students. They left out that part about the eyeball class.

Chapter 70

I never asked what a termination procedure would look like. I read that some Christian faiths were in favour of 'induction' when severe abnormalities were detected. Not exactly an abortion, but you force the baby out when he/she can't possibly survive outside the womb. It's not the chop and vacuum procedure on the Right to Life signs but the result is the same. The theory was that if you waited for an in utero death, you may miss out on seeing the baby breathe or blink or move.

These were a few of the incentives of termination. There was also a mortality-based myth that if the baby dies, he/she would not spontaneously deliver and if left for more than two weeks, the material that is shared between mother and baby would become toxic and would start killing the mother.

While we waited for an answer that took 7 weeks, my favourite place to get my breath was on the floor at the foot of my bed. It's where I spent a lot of time when the nausea, anxiety and exhaustion got overwhelming. I wasn't praying. It had just become comfortable and took pressure off my back although maybe I squeezed out a "what the fuck God?" from time to time. I was grateful to have been given the opportunity to terminate. I knew I had an absolute out from this horrific nightmare. It made it easier to breathe when felt like I was underwater with a big heavy shoe on my neck. It was perhaps the most helpless I've ever felt and choosing to continue the pregnancy was my gift to Joe. I couldn't find doctors who would operate on him and I certainly couldn't fix what was wrong but I could do this noble thing and keep carrying him. The stories I've heard from women who chose to terminate did not make those decisions lightly and in terms of the impact, they are no better or worse off than I turned out. We all lost.

Chapter 71

The folks I talked about in this book - Dr. Porter, Michele, my mother-in-law, Dr. Eyeball, PervyTrousers, the dirt mothers - they are all highly intelligent people who I believe simply lacked awareness. Not just towards me but overall for them to have missed an opportunity to ease someone's pain I suspect they were just oblivious to their own ability or power. My mother-in-law, for example, gave me many distractions at the most inopportune times or perhaps at the best times. They all did. It was someone to yell at, someone to blame for a senseless unfair loss.

Maybe I deserved to lose Joe but Cole didn't. Josh didn't either. And Connor deserved a mom that wasn't broken before he even arrived.

I want to tell Joe's story because I believe the complications and distractions are the hardest parts. Lots of people lose babies. Yeah but were they survivors of sexual abuse? Did they get out of an abusive marriage? Did they have a mean professor? I mean poor little Vickie, how awful, someone sent her flowers. Tsk. Tsk. All I had to do was refuse the deliveries. My story is no more tragic than the next guy.

I guess I wanted people who are going through this to know that it's perfectly normal to think of other things when this happens. The bills, the shitty job, the thing that didn't work out in high school. That's grief. You need things to rail against. It doesn't mean you aren't thinking about the right things or not missing your child. It halts your life. It's a freeze frame in a stop motion movie. You notice the dirty fingerprints on Rudolph's feet. You see Santa's beard falling off. You see the part of the scenery that doesn't completely cover up what's behind the curtain. It reveals life's imperfections and makes it harder to suspend disbelief. There is grief behind the curtain. Only a few of us get a glimpse of that. What a relief that we don't all see it at the same time.

Chapter 72

A note from Dad

As I read this story, the story of our lives so far, I am reminded that my wife is equally hard on herself and easy on me. What I remember during most of the chapters in this book is how helpless, useless, and numb I felt through a difficult and scary chapter in our relationship. Think about any of the scenes that Vickie described in our story. If you look hard enough, probably right around the corner or outside the bedroom door, you might see a rather pitiful and scared man-child stuck between action and inaction. I was that "friend" that just didn't know what to say or do. I wanted to help, I just didn't know how.

There are a couple times in the book where she says that this happened to us or that the ones affected the most in this type of story are the mother, the father, and the siblings. That might be somewhat misleading. First, there's the mother. Then, way on down the line, and I mean so far you can hardly see them, there's the rest of the immediate family. We're there, we're involved, but I don't think we entertain any illusion that this is something that's happening to us too.

It's heartbreaking to see someone that we love so much go through something so hard. So we just give her hugs. Or wait until it's okay to give her hugs. And we get through another day. Until the days are easier to get through and we realize that we're just a different kind of family, like a jigsaw puzzle with a missing piece. No, that's not a good analogy - it's more like walking into a room and smelling the perfume of someone you love that had just been there. Even though they aren't there anymore, it still makes you smile to think about them.

One thing I remember pretty clearly about that winter was the day we decided to buy the baby clothes. The three of us were driving to Portland and we were having a positive, uplifting conversation - you know the kind - we were deciding to look ahead with hope, despite what the doctors and nurses and ultrasound technicians were saying, despite how easy it was to feel hopeless, and despite how much we were hurting all the time. We made the decision to move forward, one day at a time, and treat this pregnancy like any other exciting, beautiful life-changing miracle, and no matter what we would love our baby more than any person had ever been loved before.

Being scared was hard. Mentally preparing for whatever was going to happen was hard. But being positive and picturing a baby that we made, crawling around and getting on Cole's nerves and just being in our lives, that made things a little bit easier.

The stuff that happened after that conversation was tough. Again, I am not deluded enough to think that I know just how tough it was for Vickie, but we did our best to stay positive. Some days were more difficult than others. We focused on our family and we did what we needed to do to get through. And now we're on, what, the other side? We lost one of our boys. We still have each other and two little people running around our house. A lot of loss families don't have nearly that much. But there's always something. Something positive to hold on to, even if it is just that idea of your sweet little creation looking over you and wishing you a happy life. Find that something and hold on to it until it hurts a little less. Even if it doesn't feel like it - everything is going to be okay.

Chapter 73

Thank You

Thank you to my partner for being my partner in every sense of the word. And for editing this book to ensure it was somewhat coherent for others going through the same thing.

Thank you to all my boys for letting me try out my parenting ideas and making my life infinitely better. You are truly my best friends.

To Gail - your name is in my book 20 times. How do I ever thank you for what you did for me? I'm sorry I wasn't able to maintain our friendship.

To Olivia - for attending deliveries like Joe's; for posing my son's body in the hospital pictures so that I'd see the beauty I missed in the delivery room; for catching him and holding him until the doctor arrived. I'm so grateful you were there.

To the 51 people on Facebook who have consistently liked my status updates and posts about Joe these past five years - thank you for making it okay to not be okay.

Thank you also to Jos, Millie, Josée, Gladys, Albert, Russell, Pete, Nicole, Amber, Deborah, Danielle, Lisa, Joanna, Janice, Todd, Jay, Andi, Caroline, LaVelle, Leevada, Toney, Anna, Jeremy, Kim, Blayne, Kelly, Steven, Della, Chrissy, Joanne, Bev, Sheila, Lynn, Fr. Al, Angela, Lois, Jody, Mary Elizabeth, Angie, Susan, Janet, Tim, Cortney, Felecia, Jason, Sean, Andrea, Nick, April, Darrin, Gina, Noel, Jaime, Aiden, Pat, Glen, Mandy, Tanya, Renee, Matthew, Coreena, Sara, Ashley, Katherine, Dawn, Megan, Craig, Geoff, Maria, Erica, Greg, Cathy, Kathy, Jonathan, Gabe, Randi, Sarah, Dionne, Denise, Jennifer, Pamela, Margaret, Courtney, Violet, Melissa, Tara, Arch, Mike, Gerry, Jamie, Will, Marjorie, Barb, Michelle, Terri, Tom, Alan, Daphne, Corey, Petrina, Emma, Rudy, Brendan, Steve, June, Samantha, Krista, Sue, Kent, Connie, Vickie, Nancy, Diane, Crystal, Brian... thank you all for trusting that the only wrong thing to say is nothing.

And thank *you* for allowing Joe and me into your space.

Chapter 74

I started writing this book on December 28, 2017 - the anniversary of the day we had the ultrasound on Joe. I was shut down for most of December not wanting to put up a tree or cook a turkey or listen to Christmas music. It had been five years already. We had uprooted and moved to Canada and I found a room in the house that seemed to say "You can write in here."

I worried about how I would close off this book a few weeks back and Cole walked into the kitchen asking what was wrong. That kid can tell from across the room if something is bothering me and he is instantly drawn to fix it. I said I don't know what to write for the ending.

Cole thought about it for a second and asked "It's about Joe right?"

Yes Cole, the book is about your brother Joe.

How about you tell people 'We didn't want to bury Joe in the ground and that's why we loved him enough to cremate him and now we get to keep him with us.'

He's already got a better grasp on this than I ever will.

I agonized over whether I should share this story and it was Josh and Cole and Connor who kept encouraging me. This is our story. Joe is and will continue to be an important part of all of our lives.

I have been having flashbacks and reliving the loss of my son each year that he has been gone. Maybe next year will be easier.

There is healing in sharing and I am so grateful for those who have gone before me that wrote their stories and published them or put them online. You will never know the comfort it provided to know we weren't alone in our darkest, 4 am nightmares. Or perhaps you did. And to you, reading this, I hope you tell your story. Our babies matter. Our pain matters. You are not alone.

I just looked at the clock. I couldn't bear the thought of another night of editing or writing and felt compelled to get this finished. It's 2:06 am, February 12, 2018. Right about now five years ago I was getting up to go to the bathroom. I'm here Joe. I'm open. And I'm ready for whatever comes next.

~Vickie

www.ingramcontent.com/pod-product-compliance
Lightning Source LLC
Chambersburg PA
CBHW030824090426
42737CB00009B/857